NORBERT ZIMMERMANN

THE FORGOTTEN PASSENGERS OF THE TITANIC - FOREVER THIRD CLASS

"On the TITANIC, even a dog had a better chance of survival than a third-class passenger!"

Bibliographic information of the German National Library

The German National Library lists this publication in the German National Bibliography; detailed bibliographic data are available on the Internet at http://dnb.d-nb.de.

ISBN: 978-3-8192-4443-8

Cover image: David Oliveira

Publisher: BoD · Books on Demand GmbH, Überseering 33, 22297 Hamburg, bod@bod.de
Printer: Libri Plureos GmbH, Friedensallee 273, 22763 Hamburg

MIX
Papier aus verantwortungsvollen Quellen
Paper from responsible sources
FSC® C105338
FSC
www.fsc.org

CONTENTS

THE AUTHOR

Author Norbert Zimmermann, born in 1970, has been researching the history of TITANIC for almost four decades and is considered one of Germany's leading TITANIC experts. He has been a welcome guest speaker at TITANIC conventions abroad. He is also the historical advisor for the TITANIC musical at Theater Osnabrück and the European coordinator of the British Titanic Society (BTS).

INTRODUCTION

The tragic sinking of the RMS TITANIC on her maiden voyage has lost none of its fascination to this day. The stories of the passengers of the legendary luxury liner are both moving and sad. But even 110 years after the sinking, more is known about the famous first-class passengers, such as John Jacob Astor, Mr. and Mrs. Straus and Benjamin Guggenheim, than about the third-class passengers, the so-called "steerage".

At that time, the general public was more interested in the VIP passengers than in the many nameless third-class passengers. And so many tragic fates tend to remain unknown. This can also be seen from the fact that only a few third-class passengers, such as Daniel Buckley, were questioned by the two committees of inquiry following the terrible tragedy. After the disaster, the newspapers of the time also focused more on the alleged heroic deeds of the prominent passengers (although many of these so-called "heroic deeds" were invented by the press) than on the fate of the poor third-class passengers. With 708 passengers, third class was the largest group on board after the crew (891 passengers). And only 180 of them survived the sinking. Many extended families who travelled in third class went down with the TITANIC.

In this book, I would like to bring some of the fates of the third-class passengers back into our memories, because they are also worth telling for future generations.

For example, the incredibly sad story of the "Addergoole 14", which until a few years ago was as good as forgotten even in its home village, or the fate of the "Longford Girls" and many more.

I hope I can help to preserve the legacy of these people with this book.

Norbert Zimmermann
March 2025

FOREWORD BY COMMODORE RONALD WARWICK

In 1912, the ill-fated TITANIC called at Cobh on her maiden voyage. Amongst those joining the liner were fourteen passengers from Addergoole who had decided to leave their families, relatives and friends in search of a better life in the distant land of America.

This group of passengers from County Mayo, have become known as the "Addergoole 14" and this book sets out to tell us more about them as individuals, their reasons for leaving home and their hopes for the future.

Undoubtebly, there would have been some tears shed as they departed from their homeland but any sadness would have soon given way to thoughts of life ahead and the excitement of being on board the newest and most modern steamer afloat.

As we all know, the lives of so many ended abruptly in the freezing waters of the North Atlantic but three of this Irish group survived. They survived to tell stories of the sinking, like many others of which are told in this book.

Frequently it takes a disaster with the loss of life to improve conditions for those left behind. Most certainly this was the case for all those aboard TITANIC - passengers and seafarers alike. As sad as it was, those who died did not do so in vain.

The tragedy made lifes safer for those travelling by sea. More safety regulations were introduced which included the provision of adequate lifeboat capacity for all on board and the International Ice Patrol was established.

The British Titanic Society serves to perpetuate the memory of those that were lost and I congratulate member Norbert Zimmermann for this written memorial to them.

Commodore R W Warwick OBE
President - British Titanic Society

THE THIRD CLASS OF THE TITANIC

Like many other ships of the time, the TITANIC was a ship designed to transport as many emigrants as possible.

A few years earlier, the third class on ships, also known as steerage, was little more than a cargo hold in which the poor emigrants were packed. It was more like a cattle transport.

The fact that epidemics and diseases spread was of course no coincidence.

The White Star Line decided to change this and take a different approach.

By also providing a minimum level of comfort for third class, they managed to build up a very good reputation in emigrant circles, so that many emigrants preferred the ships of the White Star Line. And in times of large waves of emigrants from Europe, this was a very profitable business.

And so, the company began to gradually improve the facilities, accommodation and catering in third class.

Of course, the furnishings were rather spartan compared to first and second class, but compared to other shipping companies, third class on the TITANIC (or the OLYMPIC) was downright luxurious and probably comparable to second class on many other competitor`s ships, which were also only slowly coming round to the idea of adapting third class to more modern requirements.

On the Olympic class ships (OLYMPIC, TITANIC and later BRITANNIC), the third class had its own lounge equipped with benches, tables and chairs and a piano for communal song evenings.

The walls were clad in pine wood with enamel decorations and the furniture was made of teak.

Third class also had a smoking room (not as grand as in first and second class, of course), which was furnished with oak paneling and teak furniture.

The dining room was rather plainly furnished, although the chairs were a better alternative than the usual bolt-on benches.

The hall was 30.5 meters long and took up the entire width of the ship, offering space for 470 passengers.

The fact that they were served several substantial meals a day was completely unusual for third-class passengers.

There was a very extensive breakfast, a multi-course lunch menu (starter soup, usually a vegetable soup), a main course (consisting of potatoes, vegetables and meat, followed by fruit), a kind of small tea time (simple pastries with a choice of tea, hot milk or hot cocoa) and a sumptuous evening meal for third class passengers with a final hot milk or hot cocoa.

Further evidence of the extremely good cuisine and catering is the fact that a piece of meat was served on board "every day". Surviving stewards later reported that some third-class passengers wanted to get up after the first course of soup because they thought that was already the main meal and had to be informed that the main meal would be served after the soup.

Due to the limited capacity of the dining room, there were two meal sessions in a row, half an hour apart.

The White Star Line also came up with a very good marketing idea: Each menu card could also be used as a postcard on the reverse so that emigrants, who wanted to catch up with their families who had stayed at home as soon as possible, could send these cards as proof of the opulent meals on board.

The message's aim was clear: if the meals were so good and opulent in third class, then the remaining family should also emigrate on a White Star Line steamer if possible.

Most of the cabins in third class had four or six beds. The unmarried men and women were accommodated separately on opposite sides of the ship.

In many families, fathers were only accommodated with their sons and mothers only with their daughters.

A replica of a third-class cabin © private photo of the author

In conclusion, it should be noted that the third-class facilities and catering on the TITANIC were exceptionally good for a ship of that time.

BARRIER IN THE MIND

When the terrible sinking of the TITANIC was made public, the world was absolutely shocked. After all, the TITANIC had been considered the safest ship in the world and was "unsinkable". And then it sank on its maiden voyage with 2208 people on board.

The first reports of the disaster were very unclear. The "New York Times "was the first newspaper that announced that the TITANIC had sunk. And that was before this announcement was officially confirmed by the White Star Line. Based on the facts available to them, the editors of the "New York Times" were absolutely correct in concluding that the abrupt interruption of radio communication with the TITANIC at 2:17 a.m. shipboard time allowed only one conclusion to be reached: The TITANIC had sunk!

When the report was confirmed, the newspapers went into overdrive, outbidding each other with speculation about what might have happened. They only had the radio communications between the sinking TITANIC and other ships and the most fantastic stories were created from this information. Basically, nothing was known, but the newspaper readers wanted to hear stories. And the prominent passengers on board were important. What about the Astors? Or Benjamin Guggenheim? Or the many other VIPs on board the ship?

The captain of the CARPATHIA, Arthur Henry Rostron, had only released the most necessary information to the public - that the TITANIC had sunk and that the CARPATHIA would come to New York with the survivors. Even a request from the American President William Howard Taft, who inquired about his friend and military advisor Major Archibald Butt, remained unanswered.

The captain of the CARPATHIA, Arthur Henry Rostron, became a hero by saving the TITANIC survivors © Library of Congress

Due to a lack of information, many newspapers began to invent their own stories about the tragic sinking of the luxury liner.

True heroic deeds by the prominent passengers of the luxury liner. Many of these stories have survived until today.

When the CARPATHIA finally arrived in New York in the evening hours of April 18, 1912 with only 712 survivors of the TITANIC, the press was very creative. Some newspapers had chartered boats that sailed up to the CARPATHIA as the "American Press Boat" and called over financial offers to the TITANIC survivors so that they would be available for interviews.

You can see from this front page of the New York Times from Wednesday, April 17, 1912, that only the prominent passengers on board the TITANIC were actually of interest to readers. © public domain

But hardly anyone was interested in one group of passengers: the third-class passengers!

It is undisputed and can be proven by the bare figures that the third-class passengers of the TITANIC from the

17

so-called „steerage" suffered by far the most deaths after the crew.

But what was the reason for this? Why were there so many victims in third class? There are many reasons.
The scenes from James Cameron's 1997 blockbuster "TITANIC", in which third-class passengers are explicitly shown standing in front of locked and heavily guarded gates in narrow staircases and are not allowed to go upstairs, while the crew members ask them to please remain calm, are deeply engraved in our collective memory.

There is only one catch to these scenes: the TITANIC's construction plans do not show such barriers, which could have blocked the third-class passengers' escape route up to the boat deck.

The construction plans only show barriers in the bow area near the mail rooms and in the stern area near the crew and storage rooms.

However, according to survivors from third class, there were indeed some barriers where passengers from steerage were held back by the crew.

An example of this is the story of the young, 17-year-old Irish girl Kate Gilnagh (see also chapter: "The Longford Girls"). On her way to the boat deck, she and her three friends stood in front of a locked iron gate and tried to persuade a sailor to open it. But the sailor stubbornly refused, until Kate Gilnagh's compatriot Jim Farrell got fed up and shouted at the sailor in a powerful voice:

"For heaven's sake! Open the gate and let these girls through."

The resolute and harsh tone broke the seaman's resistance, so that he finally opened the gate and let the four girls through.

Daniel Buckley also reported to the American committee of inquiry that the third-class passengers were held back by barriers and parts of the crew:

Daniel Buckley:

"Yes; they did. There was one steerage passenger there, and he was getting up the steps, and just as he was going in a little gate a fellow came along and chucked him down; threw him down into the steerage place. This fellow got excited, and he ran after him, and he could not find him. He got up over the little gate. He did not find him."

Senator Smith:

„What gate do you mean?"

Daniel Buckley:

"A little gate just at the top of the stairs going up into the first-class deck."

Senator Smith:

"There was a gate between the steerage and the first-class deck?"

Daniel Buckley:

"Yes. The first-class deck was higher up than the steerage deck, and there were some steps leading up to it; 9 or 10 steps, and a gate just at the top of the steps."

Senator Smith:

"Was the gate locked?"

Daniel Buckley:

"It was not locked at the time we made the attempt to get up there, but the sailor, or whoever he was, locked it. So that this fellow that went up after him broke the lock on it, and he went after the fellow that threw him down. He said if he could get hold of him he would throw him into the ocean."[1]

If you read through this statement, Buckley does not seem to be describing a grille inside the ship, but rather a small gate on the forward well deck of the ship from which you could access the first-class deck.

However, there were a number of barriers or gates in third class, but not to confine passengers.

There was a gate at the front of third class where the stairs led up to the open third-class room on the starboard side, but this would not have locked anyone in as there was a corridor aft from this room and this gate was only used on the port side.

---

[1] Testimony of Daniel Buckley at the American inquiry on Friday, May 3, 1912

Another door was located far aft beyond Scotland Road at the entrance to third class.

There may also have been two on Scotland Road in third class, but these only closed where the stairs descended into the third-class dining room and may only have been used when the dining room was not in use and was being prepared for the next session to prevent passengers walking in.

When all the facts are put together, it cannot be completely ruled out that third-class passengers were restrained by crew members or at gate bars. Even if there were no explicit gates holding back third-class passengers in the TITANIC's construction plans.

Another, much more serious problem that led to the exorbitantly high number of victims is undoubtedly the construction of the ship and also the language problem of a large number of the passengers in steerage.

A fairly large number of people on steerage, often with their children or even babies in tow, came from all over the world and very few spoke English. As a result, the crew's instructions and the signs in English were often not understood.

The strict separation of classes on board the ship, due to American immigration laws, also made it almost impossible for third-class passengers to get to the boat deck quickly.

Some of the families were located in different areas of the ship and it simply took far too long for them to be reunited and make their way to the potentially rescuing boat deck together. By the time they got there, most of the boats had already been launched and the chance of rescue was gone.

Some of the surviving officers later reported how horrified and stunned they were when, shortly before the TITANIC sank, a huge crowd of third-class passengers suddenly came out of the stairwells and onto the boat deck. They had actually assumed that they had gotten most of the passengers into the boats. But that had not been the case.

And probably the biggest problem was the barrier in people's minds, who simply didn't dare to take the initiative and try to save themselves because of their status in society. They waited for instructions, as they were used to doing, and simply did not dare to break out of this habitual pattern.

Some third-class survivors later reported how large groups of passengers prayed the rosary together and waited for help from above instead of trying to save themselves.

Some of the third-class passengers, when the hopelessness of their situation became obvious to them, went back to their cabins to wait for the end and go down with the ship.

It also seems to be the case that, as the late German author Wolf Schneider once put it in a TITANIC documentary: "Nobody was interested in the third-class passengers!"

There is only talk of a steward who was sent to third class by Captain Smith to take them upstairs. One group seemed to have made it, but when this steward went down again to bring another group up, he didn't seem to have made it in time, because he was never seen again!

So, it is not surprising that so few third-class passengers survived the sinking of the TITANIC.

Another highly controversial point is whether the officer's used guns against passengers and whether there were any fatalities.

It is known that Fifth Officer Harold Lowe fired several warning shots along the side of the ship. However, it has been vehemently denied that passengers were also shot.

However, there are numerous statements that challenge this belief. Here is a small selection from which you can see that third-class passengers were also very badly affected:

"You get very serious when you've experienced something so terrible... I feel as if I can still hear the cries for help today. And some were shot while trying to board the boats."

(Karl Albert Midtsjo, April 19, 1912)

„On the side where I was carried, some wild-looking men were trying to rush into the boats, and the officers and crew fired at them. Some of the men fell. Others were beaten back by the officers who used their pistols on them."

(Miss Margaret Mannion, Chicago American, Tuesday, April 23, 1912)

"Just then I saw another boat nearby being loaded preparatory to going in the water. It was nearly full of women when I saw a man try to get in. The sailors held him back but he managed to break thru them and jumped into the boat. When he stood up a sailor pulled out a revolver and shot him. The man's body tumbled over the side of the boat and that was the last I saw of him. "

(Miss Mariayam Nakid, Waterbury Republican, Thursday, April 25, 1912)

"I recall that I was pushed along toward one of the boats and helped in. The boat was lowered part way down on the davits. Just as we were about to clear the ship, a man made a rush to get aboard and was shot. He was apparently killed instantly and his body fell into the boat at our feet. No one made an effort to move the body, and it remained beneath our feet until we were picked up by the Carpathia."

(Lady Lucy Christiana Duff-Gordon, New York Herald, Friday, April 19, 1912)

"When the steerage passengers came up many them had knives, revolvers and clubs and sought to fight their way to the two unlaunched, collapsible boats. Many of these were shot by the officers"

(Dr. Washington Dodge, San Francisco Bulletin, Saturday, April 20, 1912)

THIS STATEMENT SEEMS TO REFLECT A GENERAL DISLIKE AND DISRESPECT FOR THIRD-CLASS PASSENGERS. ...

24

„An officer pointed a revolver and said if any man tried to get in, he would shoot him on the spot. I saw the officer shoot two men dead because they tried to get into the boat. Afterwards there was another shot, and I saw the officer himself lying on the deck. They told me he shot himself, but I did not see him."
(Mr. Eugene Patrick Daly)

"As the excitement began, I saw an officer of the Titanic shoot down two steerage passengers who were endeavoring to rush the lifeboats. I have learned since that twelve of the steerage passengers were shot altogether, one officer shooting down six. "(Dr. Washington Dodge)

It seems that here, too, the third-class passengers' social standing was their ruin.

If you then consider, for example, that the fifth officer Harold Lowe referred to the third-class passengers as cowards or "Italians" after the disaster (for which he later had to apologize to the Italian ambassador to the USA), you get a rough idea of how the steerage passengers were thought of and what status they had.

Two TITANIC lifeboats on their way to the CARPATHIA ©
Library of Congress

After the disaster, an infinite number of third-class
women were left with absolutely nothing, because their
husbands and thus the breadwinners of the family had
gone down with the TITANIC and the women were left
alone and completely destitute with their children.

And very few people were interested in their fate. The
press preferred to report on the first class and their
supposed heroic acts rather than on the many victims
from the third class. That was just a statistic. It was
noticeable that there were a lot of victims, including
children, but no one really took any notice.

First class passengers George & Dorothy Harder in conversation with Sallie Beckwith © Library of Congress

A group of survivors of the TITANIC aboard the CARPATHIA © Library of Congress

It was only after years that TITANIC historians brought many of the terrible stories of the third-class passengers out of forgetfulness.

One of the most shocking stories is the story of the British Goodwin family, which included eight family

27

members. In search of a better life, they boarded the TITANIC in Southampton. All eight lost their lives in the tragedy. The Goodwins' youngest son - Sidney Goodwin - was just 19 months old.

His body was found and recovered after the disaster, but remained unidentified and went down in the history books as "the unknown child". It was not until almost 100 years after the sinking of the TITANIC that the identity of little Sidney could be clarified through DNA analysis. He is buried - alongside 120 other TITANIC victims - at Fairview Cemetery in Halifax.

The gravestone of Sidney Goodwin at Fairview Cemetery in Halifax © private photo Norbert Zimmermann

The story of Margaret Rice and her five children is another tragic example of the fates that unfolded on the TITANIC. Margaret was a widow who wanted to travel to America with her children to start a new life there. But when the TITANIC sank, they all died together in the icy waters of the North Atlantic. The disaster was particularly dramatic for many of the families on board because they did not want to be separated from each other.

The surviving wireless operator Harold Bride is carried off the CARPATHIA with frozen feet © Library of Congress

Women and girls often had the opportunity to board a lifeboat, as the rule "women and children first" applied. However, the male members of the family - fathers, brothers and often underage boys - had to stay behind on the ship. On the White Star Line, boys aged 12 and over were considered "men".

This meant that they were not allowed in the lifeboats and had to stay on board, even though they were actually still children.

Many families therefore decided to stay together rather than leave their fathers or older boys behind.

This clearly shows how difficult it was for large families on board the TITANIC to survive the sinking. In principle, it was practically impossible.

LEO ZIMMERMANN - THE FARMER FROM THE BLACK FOREST

When Germans are mentioned on board the TITANIC, it is usually Alfred Nourney, Father Joseph Peruschitz or Alfred Theissinger. One German passenger is usually more or less forgotten: the third-class passenger Leo Zimmermann.

The story of Leo Zimmermann, who was 29 years old at the time of the sinking of the TITANIC, is worth telling, even if there is unfortunately not much information about him.

His last known place of residence was the peaceful village of Todtmoos in the Black Forest, where he worked as a farmer. The Zimmermann family was quite large - Leo had a total of nine siblings - five brothers and four sisters. His father Josef earned his livelihood as a sales representative.

Life in the country was difficult for the family and it became even more difficult when the family's 150-year-old house burned down in 1900 and the family lost almost all their belongings.

When the family had slowly recovered from this, the next heavy blow of fate hit them when Leo's mother Ludwina died in 1905.

Leo Zimmermann did not see any good perspectives for his future in imperial Germany and so he decided to realize his long dream of the New World. His two brothers Edwin and Arnold had already emigrated to the region of Saskatoon, Saskatchewan in Canada and Leo wanted to follow them.

Leo made all the arrangements for his big move to Canada and said goodbye to his family. Nobody could have known that Leo would never arrive in Canada.

In those days, people did not simply book a passage on a specific ship of their choice, but instead turned to an agency, as in the case of Leo Zimmermann to Kaiser & Cie. in Basel (other sources speak of Zurich), where he bought a ticket for 390 Swiss francs for a trip across the Atlantic. The agency liked to put together travel groups and so the German Leo Zimmermann ended up in a group with the Swiss Anton Kink and his family.

While researching this book, an interesting detail emerged: There exists a passenger list of the OLYMPIC from Wednesday, April 3, 1912, on which the clearly legible name Leo Zimmermann has been crossed out. The note that Leo Zimmermann was a German is also clearly visible.

It is very likely that the crossed-out German passenger Leo Zimmermann is the later TITANIC passenger, even though the name Zimmermann is widely used in the German-speaking world.

But it would indeed be a very big coincidence if the crossed-out passenger Leo Zimmermann from Germany was not the later TITANIC passenger.

A historical postcard of the OLYMPIC © authors collection

Whether the White Star Line simply made a mistake and then corrected it by simply crossing out the name, or whether Leo Zimmermann was really supposed to travel on the OLYMPIC, cannot be verified anymore.

But at least the later TITANIC passenger Leo Zimmermann boarded the TITANIC a week later in Southampton under ticket number 315082.

Clearly recognizable: The crossed-out name of Leo Zimmermann on the passenger list of the OLYMPIC from Wednesday, April 3, 1912 © ancestery.co.uk

LEO ZIMMERMANN IS NOT THE ONLY PASSENGER WHO SEEMINGLY GOT REBOOKED FROM THE OLYMPIC, AS THE FIRST-CLASS PASSENGER WILLIAM CARTER. CARTER WAS AN AMERICAN BUSINESSMAN AND OWNER OF THE RENAULT MADE FAMOUS BY JAMES CAMERON'S "TITANIC" WHEN JACK AND ROSE SPENT THEIR FIRST AND ONLY NIGHT TOGETHER IN IT. CARTER HAD ALSO INITIALLY BOOKED A PASSAGE ON THE OLYMPIC. HE AND HIS ENTIRE FAMILY WERE SUPPOSED TO BOARD THE OLYMPIC ON APRIL 3, 1912, BUT WERE THEN REBOOKED ON THE TITANIC.

Leo Zimmermann shared cabin E58 on the TITANIC, which had six beds, with the brothers Anton and

34

Vincenz Kink, Joseph Arnold and Wenzel Linhart, among others.

When the ship hit the iceberg, the men tried to escape their tragic fate later that night, but only Anton Kink managed to get into a lifeboat (number 2).
All the others from cabin E58 died, including Leo Zimmermann, and his body was never found.

Father Josef and his brother Matthäus received final certainty about Leo's fate when they received confirmation of his death on the TITANIC on Tuesday, June 4, 1912 from the Grand Ducal District Office in St. Blasien.

The idyllic St. Blasien in Baden-Würtemberg in Germany. © Martina Seeberg

Two months later, the family asserted claims for damages, including reimbursement of the cost of his TITANIC tickets and compensation of 8050 Reichsmark for his father Joseph Zimmermann, whose living expenses Leo had allegedly paid.

The statement of claim states:

"Let us also add that the father and all the siblings are poor people and that the sum requested is certainly low."

On Tuesday, April 8, 1913, almost a year after the tragedy, the family received a reply:

"According to a communication from the Imperial Consulate General in London, the application of Matthäus Zimmermann in Todtmoos has not been considered."

Only father Joseph Zimmermann was awarded an amount of 805.35 Reichsmark. A small amount for the loss of a human life.

For many years, Leo Zimmermann's fate was completely forgotten until a few years ago, when a lost letter from Swiss passenger Anton Kink surfaced. Apart from the fact that he shared cabin E58 with Leo, he was also part of the same group traveling from Basel to Southampton.

The letter was addressed to the emigration agency Kaiser & Cie in Basel, and in its Kink reported on the inconvenience of the journey to Southampton, with long waits on the train and poor catering. Kink also reported how on the ship that transported the group from Le Havre to Southampton, they were crammed into a large cabin with 40 or more beds, in which many passengers became seasick. It was only on the TITANIC that the group enjoyed their voyage, with good food and comfortable cabins, although they were accommodated separately by gender. Leo, Anton Kink and his brothers shared the six-bed cabin E-58 with Joseph Arnold and Wenzel Linhart.

Kink describes how the men experienced the collision:

"On Sunday night we went to bed comfortably, not suspecting anything dangerous, and we were sleeping soundly when at 11:45 a.m. a terrible blow and a roar roused us from sleep, and at that moment the whole ship came alive. We were partially dressed and went out on the foredeck and saw a lot of ice. We also saw steam being let off and when I asked what had happened, I was told that the Titanic had hit an iceberg but there was no danger and to calm down and go back to the cabin. Several people told me this and also emphasized that "the TITANIC cannot sink" [2]

Kink describes how difficult the journey to a lifeboat was, even for a family with a baby. The family struggled through a crowded maze of corridors and stairwells to even get to the deck. Once there, the woman and child were allowed to board a boat, but one of the crew members made it clear: no men! Kink kept an eye on his family, and when the sailors were distracted, he slipped through the barricade and made it off the ship 35 minutes before it sank.

---

[2] Quote from Anton Kink's letter to Kaiser&Cie in Basel

Whether Leo Zimmermann was ever able to get on deck or whether he had to wait for his death in front of closed doors because he was denied access to the upper decks will probably never be known...

Today there are hardly any references to Leo Zimmermann. It is known that Leo was a founding member of the musicsociety on Todtmoos-Weg and there is a photo from 1899 in which he can be seen with a trumpet.

In September 2020, on the initiative of the Titanic Society Switzerland and the municipal administration of Todtmoos, a memorial plaque was erected in honor of Leo, so that after more than a hundred years, Leo Zimmermann can finally be remembered in his hometown

The memorial plaque for Leo Zimmermann in Todtmoos © Authors collection

THE ADDERGOOLE 14

In April 1912, 14 people from the community of Addergoole in the west of Ireland set off on the long journey to the New World. They left behind bitter poverty and hoped for a better life.

Between 1850 and 1912, over four million Irish people had left their homeland - a huge number given the country's total population of just eight million! Almost every family in Ireland had relatives abroad, mainly in the USA.

In the small community of Addergoole in the north of Mayo on the west coast of Ireland - a picturesque but very remote area between the shores of Loch Conn and the hills of Nephin - poverty and lack of prospects were very high at the beginning of the last century.

And right there, in the heart of Addergoole, lies the tiny little village of Lahardane, where only 96 people lived in 22 houses in 1912.

The driving force behind this group of 14 was the 42-year-old Catherine McGowan, who had emigrated to America at the age of 19 to live with her older sister in Cleveland, Ohio. She later moved to Chicago and found happiness there.

Over 23 years after her emigration, she returned to Lahardane as a successful and independent woman to take her 17-year-old niece Annie to America to lift her out of poverty in Ireland.

She was a prime example of a successful emigrant, as she ran a very successful boarding house in Chicago, offering newly arrived immigrants' cheap accommodation and the opportunity to settle into their new surroundings.

By this time, she had become quite a wealthy woman and now returned to Addergoole in fine clothes, with lots of money and stories of the endless opportunities available to emigrants in Chicago.

Her niece Annie was very much looking forward to her aunt's arrival, as you can see from these short words:

"Dear aunt, I'm looking forward to traveling to America. I am very happy that you are picking me up. I'm looking forward to all the new opportunities and hope to find work with your help. Love, Annie McGowan"[3]

Shortly before her crossing to Ireland, Catherine McGowan wrote to her niece:

"Dearest Annie, I hope you are well. I am writing to you because I am going to Ireland in a few weeks and am very glad to see you again. I hope you will come to America with me. It is a place worth living. America offers many opportunities, lots of work. Love, your aunt, Catherine McGowan"[4]

Immediately after her arrival, she went on a promotional tour of the community to convince as many locals as

---

[3] Waking the Titanic- TV- Documentary, 2012, Director Francis Delaney
[4] Waking the Titanic- TV- Documentary, 2012, Director Francis Delaney

possible to travel back to America with her to escape poverty in Ireland. Once they arrived in America, she wanted to get each of them a job in Chicago if they came with her.

And she was very successful in her efforts. In the end, a group of 14, with her in the lead, made their way to America - the so-called "Addergoole 14".

Annie Kate Kelly, her friend Delia Mahon, Nora Fleming and Bridget Donohue did not need much convincing to emigrate, as they had been planning to leave their homeland for some time. Catherine McGowan then gave them the final push to do it.

Also, among the "Addergoole 14" were Catherine Bourke and her husband John. They had married a year earlier, on Tuesday, January 17, 1911, and they knew that their only hope for a good life together was to emigrate. They were full of

hopes and plans for their new life and were expecting their first child to be born in America.

Catherine Bourke was close friends with Catherine McGowan and had convinced them to come with her.

In a letter to her sister Ellen, she was very excited about emigrating to America:

"Dear Ellie, I think you have already heard of my decision. On April 11th I am sailing for America with Kate McGowan. You must think I'm in distress, but I'm delighted. I made up my mind immediately. I hardly have any time and I'm busier than

ever. Kate McGowan is here. I'm going to a funeral. I have to stop now. All my love, Catherine Bourke.
PS: The name of the steamer I'm traveling on is Titanic"[5]

When she heard about the emigration plans, John's sister Mary Bourke decided to emigrate to America with them as well.

The quiet and shy Mary Mangan was also friends with Catherine McGowan and had been living in Chicago for several years. She had returned to Addergoole to tell her friends and family the good news of her impending marriage.

21-year-old Pat Canavan was a rough but very warm-hearted guy from the west of Ireland. He also joined the group along with his best friend James Flynn and his cousin Mary Canavan, who was James' stepsister.

31-year-old Bridget Delia McDermott had also decided to join the group, which also included her good friend Mary Mangan. She was planning to move to St. Louis, Missouri, to live with her cousin Mary Finnerty.

The 14 from Addergoole used the last day before their departure packing, preparing and spending time with their family.

Mary Mangan spent time with her parents before returning to America, getting married and starting her own family.

The day before leaving, Delia McDermott went with her mother to a hat store in Crossmolina to buy a hat and gloves because her mother had told her that to be considered a lady in America, she had to wear a hat. All the ladies there would wear hats. To be accepted as a lady in America, she would have to arrive in New York wearing a hat and gloves.

Bridget Donohue worked in the local store. The day before leaving, the owner's three-year-old daughter asked Bridget to send her a ring from New York. Bridget measured the girl's finger with a piece of string to determine the size and promised to send her a ring as soon as possible.

James Flynn spent the last afternoon with his sister, who was very upset that James was going away. She had been deaf since birth, and James was the only one in the family and town who could communicate with her in sign language. He promised to send her a ticket as soon as he arrived in New York so that she could follow him.

On the evening before their departure, a party known as the "American Wake" was held in the homes of the emigrants. Neighbors and friends gathered to see them off with advice and memories, laughter and tears, stories, poems. It was a very emotional affair, because it was not very likely that they would return. But the joy of their new life in America prevailed.

In the old Irish tradition, there was tea, soda bread, treacle tart, a cask of porter or even a drop of the old Irish national drink poitin, which is considered the forerunner of today's whiskey.

Ballads were sung, some of them with haunting melodies, about the departure on the ship to America and the eternal departure,

There were blessings and prayers, medals and holy water from friends and relatives to protect them on their journey. Some neighbors brought a gift: Oatmeal cakes, baked and hardened on the hot stone slab in the days before their departure, to fortify them for the journey ahead.

On this last evening in their old home, they danced until daybreak. An unforgettable farewell. No one would even suspect that most of them would no longer be alive in a week's time...

It wouldn't be TITANIC if there weren't a few myths here too. Some of the group are said to have received strange warnings before the trip:

Delia McDermott, for example, was stopped by a stranger a few days before she boarded the TITANIC, who told her that she would soon be making a journey and that it would end tragically. Hundreds would die, but she would be saved.

At the Mahon family's "American Wake," Delia Mahon's older brother Pat read from her teacup, as was the custom in many households at the time. As he looked at the formation of the drained tea leaves, he told her that there would be an accident on the way to America and she would die.

UNFORTUNATELY, HER BROTHER WAS RIGHT, BECAUSE DELIA MAHON DIED IN THE SINKING OF THE TITANIC.

On the morning of April 10, 1912, the group of 14 from Addergoole made their way to the train station in Castlebar. Ahead of them lay a 14-hour journey to Queenstown (now Cobh) to the TITANIC.

When they arrived at Castlebar station, it wasn't long before the train from Westport pulled onto the platform at 8:23am. The Midland Great Western Line took the group to Claremorris. There they changed to the train to Limerick. At 11:05 am the Great Southern and Western Train set off for Limerick where they arrived at 3:41 pm.

In Limerick they boarded the Limerick Direct train, which left at 4:42pm and arrived in Cork at 6.50pm, where they were able to board one of the hourly trains to Queenstown, where they arrived in time to organize accommodation for the night.

It was already late in the evening when they arrived in Queenstown, and their thoughts now turned to the accommodation they organized with one of the station attendants, or 'runners' as they were known, who took customers to the lodgings. By 1912, the facilities for emigrants were well developed and, in that year, around 30.000 people made their way to America.

The town of Cobh, which had been renamed Queenstown in 1849 after Queen Victoria's visit, had prospered over the previous fifty years thanks to the emigrant trade, and the handsome prices charged for accommodation meant that there was indeed good money to be made.

A large number of people from all corners of Ireland were looking for accommodation for the night, as the TITANIC would not arrive in Queenstown until the next day. Luckily, the Addergoole 14 found accommodation near St. Coleman's Cathedral, where they attended mass the next morning before departing on the TITANIC.

After Mass and breakfast, they made their way to the White Star Line office, where the passengers waited in Queenstown for the tender to embark the TITANIC.

The Titanic arrived in Queenstown at 11:30 a.m. and took a total of 113 third-class passengers on board.

In an article in the Cork Examiner the following day, a reporter described the "arrival of the TITANIC" in Queenstown:

"As one saw her esteeming slowly, a majestic monster floating, it seemed irresistibly into the harbour, a strange sense of might and power pervaded the scene… Whatever conditions the modern voyager looks for in the vessel which he selects to bear him safely over the oceans, he will find here with the acme of perfection."[6]

---

[6] Quote: Cork Examiner, Friday, April 12, 1912

From there, the TITANIC set off on her maiden voyage in Queenstown (now Cobh) on Thursday, April 11, 1912. © Private photo Norbert Zimmermann

The passengers gathered on the quay near the White Star Offices and waited to be picked up by the tender. For most of those waiting there, it was probably the first time they had ever seen the sea, a tender or a large ocean liner like the TITANIC.

Shortly after midday, the "Addergoole 14" and all their luggage were taken aboard the TITANIC in one of the dinghies.

Before departure, doctors examined the emigrants' state of health for signs of illness before issuing a clearance certificate. The same procedure was to be repeated on arrival in America. Another passenger from County Mayo, Annie Jordan from Lack, Turlough, took this procedure as a reason not to travel, as she had developed a severe rash and feared she would not be allowed to enter the country. A few days later, she would find out that she was incredibly lucky...

Even the dinghy ride was a unique experience for most of them. As they approached the huge TITANIC, it seemed like a floating palace. Third-class passenger Edward Ryan remembered it vividly:

"The tender was like a matchstick compared to her. A big door opened in her side and a gangway put out so we could all get on board. We were shown to our berths and taken to see the dining room. A little later shown where to get life belts and some other of the lifesaving gear. None of us ever thought we would soon be needing it."[7]

When the TITANIC weighed anchor for the last time at 1:30 p.m., many of the emigrants looked back one last time to their home country of Ireland, which they were to leave forever. On the poopdeck, the bagpiper Eugene Daly from Athlone played "Erin's Lament".

The days on board the TITANIC were a unique experience for the group, which they thoroughly enjoyed. There were regular meals in the large dining room, which was completely unusual for most of the steerage passengers. An incredible luxury!

After the meal, they went for a walk on the poop deck, the area of the ship that was intended for third class passengers. The lounge was also a big attraction. There

---

[7] Quote: July 9, 2002 Atlantic Bulletin/Journal of the British Titanic Society

they talked about their plans for the future as Annie Kate Kelly recalled in an interview with the "Chicago Herald" that appeared on April 25, 1912:

"The young girls would talk about what they would do in America before they were married. That is, they would talk about it when they were not scurrying around the laughing and making friends here and there with everybody and joking with stewards"[8]

The couple Catherine and John Bourke had a lot to discuss and think about how they could invest the money they had as profitably as possible. During the trip, they often saw Annie McGowan deep in conversation.

On Sunday, April 14, 1912, a party was held in the evening in the third class. With music, singing and dancing and many Irish songs, the celebration was exuberant. Nora Fleming celebrated her 24th birthday and sang many Irish songs, as she must have had a wonderful singing voice.

WHAT IS INTERESTING IN THIS CONTEXT IS THAT NORA FLEMING'S DATE OF BIRTH WAS ACTUALLY APRIL 9 AND NOT APRIL 14. APRIL 14TH WAS HER BAPTISM DATE, AS CAN BE SEEN FROM HER BAPTISM AND BIRTH RECORDS.

Catherine Bourke also gave a vocal performance and sang "Moonlight in Mayo". Annie McGowan later said that John and Catherine Bourke were very happy that

---

[8] Quote; Annie Kate Kelly, Chicago Herald, April 25, 1912

evening and danced and sang together. The party ended at 10:30 p.m. and most people retired to their cabins.

Most of them didn't even notice the collision with the iceberg:

„Most of ship`s passengers retired and I was in bed and sleeping soundly. My first knowledge that all was not well was when a steward pounded on the door and his cries awakened me. Along with other passengers I rushed out. On the decks were hysterical and shrieking men and women, though the majority were taking the reported danger as a joke. There seemed to be nothing serious and I returned to bed "[9]

Delia McDermott was asleep when the TITANIC collided with the iceberg and didn't notice anything. After being woken by a stewardess, she got dressed and went to the boat deck. A short time later, a stewardess came to the group a second time:

„We were aroused a second time, by the call of a stewardess, who told us all to dress as quickly as we could, though she did not explain what the trouble was. I was dressed and went upon the second deck. Annie McGowan was with me when I was going up the stairs, but she became separated from me at the head of the stairway and was carried by the throng over to the other side of the ship. I did not see her again until I was on the Carpathia. On the side where I was carried, some wild looking men were trying to rush into the boats, and officers and crew fired at them. Some of the men fell. Others were beaten back by the officers who used pistols on them. "[10]

---

[9] Quote: Annie Kate Kelly, Chicago Herald, April 23, 1912
[10] Quote: Delia McDermott, Chicago Herald, April 23, 1912

She got into a lifeboat early. When she realized there that she had left her precious hat behind, she remembered what her mother had said to her and went back to get it from her cabin. Fortunately, she managed to get into another boat, number 13, by jumping fifteen feet from a rope ladder into the lifeboat.

Many years later, Annie McGowan also vividly recalled the events of that night:

„Women wouldn`t leave their husbands. They were screaming and I could hear gunshots in the background. Some of the men tried to dress as women in order to be rescued and they were shot. In her lifeboat a man said: „Let me in or I`ll tip the whole lifeboat…of course, we had to let him in. "[11]

Although it was denied, the third-class passengers had the least chance of rescue, as Annie Kate Kelly reported to the "Chicago Herald" on April 25, 1912:

„The first thing they saw was the people being held back from going up the stairs to the second deck. „You see it was for fear of the excitement they (steerage) would cause to the people up there who were getting away in the lifeboats and they held them back to the last moment. "[12]

Margaret Mannion had also seen similar things:

---

[11] Source; Sarah Downey- A Tragedy`s Echo- Annie McGowan`s Story, 2004, Journal of the Addergoole Titanic Society
[12] Quote: Annie Kate Kelly, Chicago Herald, April 25, 1912

„They were stopped by a large barrier at the foot of a stairway, put there to stop steerage passengers mingling on upper decks but a few strong fellows managed to smash it down "[13]

During the night, Pat Canavan and John Bourke gathered the group to go to the boat deck. The two knew that there was a ladder to the upper deck that they had to go to. As Annie Kate Kelly walked towards the ladder, a steward she had befriended on the voyage took her by the hand and led her up the stairs without anyone stopping him:

„Here`s a chance for your life Miss Kelly "

And as one of the boats was being let down, he called out:

„Let this girl go with you. You`ve got room. Let her in "[14]

Annie Kate Kelly was later convinced that she was the last woman to leave the sinking TITANIC:

„I am positive that I was the last woman to leave the sinking „Titanic "and be rescued. There was a crowd of us standing on the second deck of the ship, with water nearly to our knees. The crew ordered me into the boat and told the others to wait and take the next boat which wouldn't be launched immediately. They were no more boats and those people died. "[15]

---

[13] Source; Margaret Mannion, Irish Independent, May 9, 1912
[14] Quote: Annie Kate Kelly, Chicago Herald, April 23, 1912
[15] Quote: Annie Kate Kelly, Chicago Herald, April 23, 1912

She got into lifeboat number 16, which was one of the last boats to be launched. Mary and Catherine Bourke had initially also found a place in this boat. But when John Bourke, a man, was refused a place in the boat, the two women got out again as they didn't want to leave John behind. That was their certain death sentence!

„I should not have been saved except for Mrs. Bourke`s refusal to leave her husband "[16]

Next to the Bourkes was James Flynn, who had been pushed back when the boats were lowered.

„…they pushed the little Flynn boy back, and cut away. It was pitiful that they wouldn`t let the boy stay on the lifeboat, and he only a child and it not full "[17]

Pat Canavan, who had brought the group of women to the boat deck, stood behind the fourth funnel and near the stern.

„As she was lowered into the lifeboat, she looked up and saw her cousin watching, holding in his hand his rosary which he raised to bless her. He was among the many that went down with the ship. "[18]

---

[16] Interview with Annie Kate Kelly, Chicago Herald, April 23. 1912
[17] Interview with Annie Kate Kelly, Chicago Herald, April 23, 1912
[18] Interview with Annie Kate Kelly, Chicago Herald, April 23, 1912

Mary Mangan and Mary Canavan made it to the boat deck with the group, but their tracks were lost forever. The same happened to Nora Fleming.

Annie McGowan made it to lifeboat number 13 with the help of a sailor she had befriended. She was very worried about her Aunt Catherine, who had previously been with the Bourkes, and was reassured by a steward who assured her that she was in another lifeboat.

In her lifeboat, Annie watched as the TITANIC sank:

„That`s when all the screaming started. It was just so terrible. The salt water and wind made my eyes start to bleed. The screams of the passengers left on the decks drifted over the water. "[19]

Annie McGowan never saw her beloved aunt again, and she believed that the lifeboat her aunt supposedly had been was sucked into a whirlpool created when the TITANIC sank, as she told the "Chicago Herald" in the Tuesday, April 23, 1912 issue:

"We were lowered and the crew started pulling the lifeboat away. It seemed scarcely two minutes later when I saw two other boats following us. I could just see them dimly, when the lights on the ship suddenly went out. Then I saw the two boats pulled back in their wake. The oarsmen struggled hard to pull them away but were too late. The two boats went down in the suction of „The Titanic "as it went down to the bottom. "[20]

---

[19] Waking the Titanic- TV- Documentary, 2012, Director Francis Delaney
[20]Quote: Annie McGowan, Chicago Herald, April 23, 1912

Only three of the Addergoole group of 14 survived the sinking of the TITANIC: Annie McGowan, Annie Kate Kelly and Delia McDermott. The remaining eleven of the Addergoole 14 lost their lives in the sinking of the huge ship.

When the three were hoisted aboard the Carpathia with the other survivors of the disaster, everything was ready for them - dry clothes, blankets, beds, hot tea, coffee and spirits.

The "Chicago Herald" reported on Annie Kate Kelly in its issue of Tuesday, April 23, 1912:

„...not a thing did Annie Kate know when she was pulled over the side of „The Carpathia ". They poured ho whiskey and raw brandy into her and buried her in blankets and hot water bottles she was that frozen. "[21]

When the CARPATHIA arrived in New York around evening on Thursday, April 18, 1912, relatives of the Addergoole group were also in the waiting crowd. Catherine Fleming waited in vain for her sister Nora, while Anthony Flynn waited in vain for his brother James and Mary Canavan. It is not known whether any other members of the "Addergoole 14" were present.

Anthony Flynn eventually asked the Red Cross for help in recovering his brother's body, but to no avail. If it was ever recovered, it could not be identified.

---

[21] Source: Chicago Herald, April 23, 1912

After the White Star Line published the list of the steerage passengers, there was still great confusion about the names of the passengers from Addergoole. It was only through a letter that Annie Kate Kelly had written to her cousin Mrs. Garvey shortly before her voyage that the identity of some of the group could be established, as the "Chicago Inter Ocean" reported on Friday, April 19, 1912.

„I am coming to America on the nicest ship in the world. And I am coming with some of the nicest people in the world too. Isn`t that just splendid? She described to her cousin these new found friends and went on to say; „They live in Chicago and I shall be able to make the entire trip with them. They have told me all about Chicago and I know that I shall like it much better than I do Ireland. "[22]

The newspaper report continues:

„ From the letter it would seem that the Burkes previously had lived in St. Louis, and that Miss Manion (Mary Managan) had made her home with them for some time. They evidently had move to Chicago quite lately which may account for the lack of inquiry for them at the offices of the White Star Company. "[23]

Catherine Bourke's sister, Ellen McHugh, had called the White Star Office in Chicago and learned the sad news of the many deaths from Lahardane.

---

[22] Source: Chicago Inter Ocean, April 19, 1912
[23] Source: Chicago Inter Ocean, April 19, 1912

Edward Mangan also contacted the White Star Line office on Friday, April 19 to inquire about his sister Mary, as she was on both the list of survivors and the list of dead!

The "Chicago Tribune" reported on this on Sunday, April 21, 1912:

„It is hard to sit here and wait, nearly a week after „The Titanic "went down and not know whether she is alive or dead. It may be that she has wired me and the message failed to reach me. "[24]

The body of Mary Mangan was found on Monday, April 22nd. It was the 61st body recovered from the water, and she was easily identified by the jewelry in her belongings. She had a gold watch with her that had a photo of her and her name "M. Mangan" engraved on the inside and outside. She had her engagement ring on her finger, which was included in the list of recovered items. Later, however, this ring was no longer recorded and remained missing forever.

She was buried at sea in her clothes and her personal belongings were handed over to her family.

The bodies of the other members of the Addergoole group were never found.

Annie Kate Kelly and Annie McGowan were taken to St. Vincent Hospital in New York with only their nightgowns, donated shoes and coats, and some money

---

[24] Quote; Chicago Tribune, April 21, 1912

for their immediate needs. Neither Annie McGowan nor Annie Kate Kelly knew of each other's rescue until they met again at the hospital, thinking they were the only ones of their group to survive. At that time, they did not know that Delia McDermott had also survived the tragedy.

Annie McGowan could not say how she was rescued, but in 1984 she told the "Chicago Herald":

„I was young and swift as a hare and when the call came for them all to go on deck, I ran away to see what this and that`s how I was saved. "[25]

During her stay at St. Vincent Hospital, Annie Kate Kelly was reportedly forced to sign a waiver of damages for the White Star Line, as she reported in an interview with the "Chicago Herald" in the Tuesday, April 23, 1912 edition:

„…in a semi-conscious state, a steamship agent guided her unsteady hand after representing to her that the paper she was signing was a railroad ticket to Chicago. „It was not until I left hospital, that I learned that I had unknowingly signed a paper which released the company from all claims for damages. "[26]

The "Chicago Daily Journal" also reported on this on Wednesday, April 24, 1912:

---

[25] Interview with Annie McGowan, Chicago Herald, 1984
[26] Source: Chicago Herald, April 23, 1912

„ I found 25 dollars pinned to my underwear this morning. I had not observed it before and it all came back to me at once that I had signed some kind of a paper in the hospital. I thought I was signing my ticket for Chicago. Four men came to my bed and told me to sign something. I couldn't write even yet I cannot feel myself. She exhibited the swollen, purple hands and arms. One of them held my hand while I wrote. I was so very tired, even that seemed an effort. Then one of the men pinned something on my clothes…I wondered why there were four men, but they said they were very witness… But I didn't leave as soon as I thought I would. It seems there was some misunderstanding about the steamship company paying the sisters of St. Vincent's Hospital where I was taken for attending me. When I finally left…it was awful to start on a journey being sick but to be almost without clothes was worse. I had a simple undergarnment, my shoes and stockings and a cloak my mother bought for me in Ireland. I had no sleeves my bare arms showed…An actress, Miss Stella Donnelly of Cincinatti took off part of her clothes and gave them to me and another girl, Miss Annie McGowan, who was the only other of seventeen girls who were saved from the steerage, cut the waist from her dress and gave me the skirt. " [27]

Delia McDermott neither gave interviews to the press nor traveled to Missouri as originally intended, but stayed on the East Coast. Initially, she was probably staying in a shelter in New York and received financial support from the Red Cross.

When Annie McGowan and Annie Kate Kelly were released from the hospital, they were put on a train to Chicago. At the train station there, they were met by Dr. Mary O'Brien-Porter from the Women's League, who

---

[27] Article of the Chicago Daily Journal, April 24, 1912

asked the mayor of the city to collect donations for the survivors. In the days and weeks that followed, the two were harassed by reporters from the Chicago Herald. Annie Kate Kelly eventually testified to the newspaper, but Annie McGowan, who went to her aunt Maggie McDermott's apartment, did not break her silence until 1984, when she gave an interview to her great-granddaughter Kris Kropp, a journalist.

The terrible traumatic experience on the TITANIC, in which she lost her aunt and many of her friends, had given her a severe nervous shock, as the "Chicago Herald" reported on Sunday, April 28, 1912:

„*They* (The McDermotts, Author`s note) *cannot say a word to Annie McGowan about anything that happened at all. They fear the child will lose her mind and Mrs. McDermott does not cry or sob, though the heart of her should burst, nor ask a question of how Kate died and what she said, but must smile and show cheer, for fear the child will lose her wits. They have the Doctor for her all the time and it`s a sad house the McDermotts have this day and all days now.* "[28]

Annie Kate Kelly didn't fare much better either, as the "Chicago American" reported on Friday, April 25:

„*Dr. Thomas J. O`Malley who attended Annie Kate Kelly thought that she would never again be normal as a result of the harrowing experience she suffered when the ship sank.* "[29]

---

[28] Source; Chicago Herald, April 28, 1912
[29] Quote; Chicago American, April 25, 1912

In Lahardane, they only found out what had happened a week later. After five days there had been rumors, but the information was inaccurate and exaggerated.

Finally, the authorities in New York had all the names. It took eight or nine days for the news that their child had not made it to America to reach a family.

Local newspapers reported on the tragedy well into May, but perhaps the most harrowing account appeared in "The Western People" on Saturday, May 4, 1912 about the loss of John and Catherine (McHugh) Bourke, Mary Bourke, Nora Fleming and Mary Mangan from the village of Carrowskeheen:

TITANIC DISASTER LAHARDANE VICTIMS

"One of the saddest sights ever witnessed in the West of Ireland was the waking of five young girls and one young man from a village near Lahardane who went down with the ill-fated Titanic. They were all from the same village and when the first news of the appalling catastrophe reached their friends the whole community was plunged into insufferable grief. They cherished for a time a remote hope that they were saved but when the dreaded news of their terrible fate arrived a feeling of excruciating anguish took place. For two days and two nights wakes were held. The photograph of each victim was placed on the bed on which they had slept before leaving home and kindred. The beds were covered with snow-white quilts and numbers of candles were lighted around. The wailing and the moaning of the people was very distressing and would almost draw a tear from a stone."[30]

---

[30] Quote: The Western People, May 4, 1912

It took Annie McGowan a very long time before she was able to lead a normal life again. The trauma she had suffered was too strong. But she managed it and went to secretarial school and got a job. Shortly afterwards, she met her husband and had three daughters with him. She lived to a ripe old age and on Tuesday, January 30, 1990, she died in Chicago at the age of 95.

Delia McDermott met her future husband John Lynch in America and lived with him in New Jersey. He worked for the Central Jersey railroad all his life. They had three children. Delia was a reserved person. She ran a boarding house on Union Street. She got up early and went to early mass. And she took care of her home and didn't like to go out. She never talked about TITANIC and died on Tuesday, November 3, 1959 in New Jersey at the age of 78.

Annie Kate Kelly moved in with her sisters. She stayed there for a while until she had regained her composure. Then she looked for a job. She lived in Chicago for nine years and worked there as a milliner. After her experience on the TITANIC, her life changed completely. She felt called to dedicate her life to God and eventually became a nun. She spent most of her life teaching. She took the name Sister Patrick Joseph. She taught at many schools in the Chicago area. Many of her students kept in touch with her after her graduation until she died on Sunday, December 28, 1969 at the age of 77.

For many decades, the tragedy of the TITANIC was not talked about in Lahardane. As a result, the fate of the "Addergoole 14" was slowly forgotten. It is only in recent years that the 14 young people from their midst who set off for America and lost their lives in the sinking of the TITANIC on April 15, 1912 have been remembered again.

A memorial service is now held annually in Lahardane on the night of April 14-15.

At 2:00 a.m. a candlelight procession runs through the village to the local church of St. Patrick where a small memorial ceremony is held. At exactly 2:20 a.m., the time of the sinking of the TITANIC, the descendants of the "Addergoole 14" ring the bell 14 times to commemorate the tragic fate of their ancestors.

The Addergoole Titanic Memorial Park was also built to commemorate the 14 people from their midst who boarded the TITANIC in Queenstown (now Cobh) on April 11, 1912.

The Addergoole 14 were:

MR. JOHN BOURKE, 42 YEARS OLD

MRS. CATHERINE BOURKE, 32 YEARS

MISS MARY BOURKE, 40 YEARS

MISS MARY CANAVAN, 22 YEARS

MR. PATRICK CANAVAN, 21 YEARS OLD

MISS BRIDGET DONOHOE, 21 YEARS OLD

MISS HONOR FLEMING, 22 YEARS

MR. JAMES FLYNN, 28 YEARS OLD:

MISS ANNA KATHERINE KELLY, 20 YEARS

MISS BRIDGET DELIA MAHON, 20 YEARS OLD

MISS MARY MANGAN, 32 YEARS

MISS BRIDGET DELIA MCDERMOTT, 31 YEARS OLD

MISS CATHERINE MCGOWAN, 42 YEARS OLD

MISS ANNA LOUISE, MCGOWAN, 17 YEARS OLD

This chapter is dedicated to them.

AUGUST WENNERSTRÖM- THE POLITICALLY PERSECUTED MAN FROM SWEDEN

In many countries at the beginning of the last century there were major social differences, and Sweden was no exception. Social democracy, communism and socialism were on the rise and demanded more rights for the working class.

The 27-year-old socialist, August Edvard Andersson, had been involved in politics from an early age and was a member of the Social Democratic Youth Club. His political activities included the publication of "Gula Faran" (The Yellow Danger) in 1905, which caused quite a stir but got him into serious trouble with the Swedish authorities. In this publication, he referred to King Oscar II as the "king of thieves" and mocked Christianity, among other things.

Some non-socialist newspapers hit back, which ultimately culminated in a lawsuit that also concerned freedom of the press. After another person took responsibility for the controversial publication of "Gula Faran", August was acquitted.

Shortly afterwards, he moved to Karlstad where he was elected to the board of Värmlands Folkblad. From 1907 to 1908 he was also briefly the editor of the magazine, before being replaced by Ivar Vennerström.

After that he worked in various print shops and newspapers in Skåne, a region in the south of Sweden.

After the controversies surrounding "Gula Faran" and the financial difficulties he had encountered during his various jobs, and also because he was still on the "blacklist" of his home country, he finally decided to leave Sweden and emmigrate to America.

August Wennerström, 22 years old (1906). © Public domain

To disguise his true identity, he took the name of his friend and successor at Värmlands Folkblad, Iver Vennerström, but spelled it with a W instead of a V. (Incidentally, Ivar Vennerström was Swedish Minister of Defense from 1932-1936).

After completing all the necessary preparations, he traveled by train to Copenhagen, then by ship, and ferry, to England, and then to Southampton, where he boarded TITANIC, on Wednesday, April 10, 1912, with ticket number 350043 under his new name August Wennerström as a Third-Class passenger.

As a large number of Swedes were traveling on TITANIC (123 Swedes were on board, 112 of them in third class), August quickly made friends with some of his countrymen on board.

He shared his cabin with his countrymen Carl Olof Jansson and Gunnar Isidor Tenglin, who had both traveled to Southampton via Esbjerg. Everything went calmly and orderly until TITANIC hit the iceberg. During the night he brought some Swedish girls to the boats before returning to the third-class smoking room:

"We wanted something to drink, but the bar was closed. Since we had nothing else to do, we got someone who could play the piano and started to dance. In the meantime, fifty Italian emigrants came in.

They had life jackets on and were carrying their luggage in bundles on their backs. They were behaving like crazy - jumping around and shouting their "Madonna". We stood in a circle around them and danced around dance around them."[31]

---

[31] Source;.townepost.com/indiana/lakes-region/unsinkable-memories-titanic

After a while, more of Wennerström's compatriots arrived in the smoking room:

"One of our friends, a man by the name of Johan Lundahl who had been home to the old country on a visit and was going back to the United States said to us, "Goodbye friends; I'm too old to fight the Atlantic." he went to the smoking room and there on a chair was awaiting his last call. So did an English lady; She sat down by the piano and, with her child on her knee, she played the piano until the Atlantic grave called them both."[32]

Shortly afterwards, he made his way up from the steerage and the stern of TITANIC was already beginning to rise out of the water:

"The water was now rising faster than before, and people were trying not to slip on the deck, which was getting steeper and steeper."[33]

August and Gunnar Isidor Tenglin also met the couple Edvard and Gerda Lindell, from Helsingborg, on the boat deck, with whom August had become friends during the voyage. They were part of the huge group of third-class passengers who only appeared on the boat deck in the final moments of the sinking. It had taken too long for most of the steerage passengers to fight their way up to the Boat Deck. Most of the boats had already departed!

---

[32] Source: www.encyclopedia-titanica.org- August Wennerström
[33] Source: www.encyclopedia-titanica.org- August Wennerström

As TITANIC sank faster and faster, the group with Wennerström, Tenglin and the Lindells fought their way up the sloping deck until it became too steep and, grasping each other's hands, slid back into the immediate vicinity of the 'Collapsible A' lifeboat.

There they also met Alma Pålsson and her four children Torborg Danira (8), Paul Folke (6), Stina Viola (3) and Gösta Leonard (2). Whilst the ship was sinking, it had simply taken too long to get the four children dressed and so Alma and her children arrived on the boat deck too late.

When TITANIC finally sank, August Wennerström tried to hold on to two of the children, but lost them when the icy water washed over the deck. Alma Pålsson and her four children did not survive the sinking. Wennerström and the others plunged into the icy North Atlantic. The two Lindells reached 'Collapsible A', but the boat capsized and they fell helplessly back into the icy sea. Together with Edvard Lindell, August made it back into the now leaking boat, but Gerda Lindell was nowhere to be seen at first.

Then she saw Wennerström in the water and grabbed her hand. Weakened by the icy cold, he was unfortunately unable to help her.

"I don't know how long I was off the boat. When I reached it again, it was full of water. My friend, Mr. Lindell, had climbed in, too. I saw Mrs. Lindell in the water and grabbed her hand, but I didn't have the strength to pull her into the boat. Mr. Lindell looked straight ahead. He did not move and said not a word. He was frozen to death. After half an hour,

my strength weakened, and I watched Mrs. Lindell go down."[34]

The bodies of the Lindell couple were never found. Edvard's body was probably lowered overboard to make the unstable boat lighter.

Gerda Lindell's wedding ring was found by the crew of the OCEANIC on Monday, May 13, 1912, when Collapsible A, which was not picked up by the CARPATHIA, was located in the North Atlantic by pure chance.

According to Wennerström, Edvard Lindell had his wife's ring in his hand when he died, then it seems to have fallen back into the boat when he was hoisted out of it.

Although the boat had been drifting around for a month, the ring miraculously could still be found in it. It was taken to New York, where White Star Line employees began to identify it. It was discovered that the ring "belonged to a Mrs. Gerda Lindell," so it was sent to the Swedish Consulate in New York.

However, the passenger list showed a passenger by the name of "Elin Lindell," but it was not possible to recognize that there was actually an Elin Gerda Lindell on the TITANIC: "*And therefore, we ask you to help us by allowing us to give you this ring, provided that you agree to investigate this matter, and if the ownership claims are to be*

---

[34] Quote; Discovery Channel: Titanic - *Anatomy of a Disaster, 1997*

determined, to locate the rightful owner and hand over her property to Mrs. Lindell via her branch in Sweden."

The letter was dated Friday, 7th June 1912, and the White Star Line stationery (it still had both the OLYMPIC and the TITANIC on its letterhead) contained the ring. In fact, they were two rings forged into each other with the engraving on the inside. A few weeks later the letter arrived in Stockholm with the appeal of the Ministry of Foreign Affairs to find the owner by publishing it in some newspapers. Gerda's brother, Nils Nilsson, was employed by the Swedish National Railways and commuted between Malmö and Gothenburg. One day when he was in Gothenburg, he noticed the call in a newspaper. He became aware and showed the article to his parents. In July 1912, Gerda's father Nils Persson received the ring in Gantorfa as his next of kin.

The night in the icy North Atlantic was almost endless and sheer horror, as August Wennerström later recalled:

"All the feeling had left us. If we wanted to know if we still had legs (or any other part) left, we had to feel down in the water with our hand. The only exercise we got was when someone gave up hope and died, whom we immediately threw overboard to give the live ones a little more space and at the same time lighten the weight of the boat."[35]

---

[35] Source: www.encyclopedia titanica-August Wennerström

Titanic's 'Collapsible A' lifeboat, found by OCEANIC, on May 13th 1912. © Public Domain.

But somehow, he managed to survive this terrible night and be rescued by CARPATHIA.

The wedding ring of Gerda Lindell was presented during the Titanic Exhibition 2010 in Wiesbaden © private photo of the author

Edvard and Gerda Lindell © Authors collection

INTERESTING FACT IN PASSING: AUGUST
WENNERSTRÖM, AS WELL AS HIS CABIN MATES
CARL OLOF JANSSON AND GUNNAR ISIDOR
TENGLIN, SURVIVED THE SINKING OF OF TITANIC!
GIVEN THE HIGH NUMBER OF THIRD-CLASS
VICTIMS, THIS IS QUITE REMARKABLE. THERE IS
ALSO A SOUVENIR PHOTO OF AUGUST
WENNERSTRÖM, GUNNAR TENGLIN, CARL OLOF
JANSSON, JOHN CHARLES ASPLUND AND EINAR

KARLSSON, ALL OF WHOM SURVIVED THE AS THIRD-CLASS PASSENGERS

After his arrival in New York, he was interviewed for an article that appeared in the Brooklyn Daily Eagle on Friday, April 19, 1912, in which he described how he had managed to survive. In the meantime, he was quartered in the Salvation Army Cadet School. There he caused a minor scandal when he accused the Lutheran immigrant home of embezzlement.

He received 25 dollars and a train ticket from the Salvation Army committee, while the Red Cross gave him 100 dollars.

August Wennerström then traveled to Chicago, where he gave lectures about his experiences on the TITANIC. In the city, he met Naomi Johnson, who, like him, was of Swedish origin. She became his great love with whom he had seven children (six sons and a daughter).

He left his old life as a publicist behind and moved to Culver, Indiana, with his wife Naomi.

His motives for moving to Culver have never been entirely clear, but when he arrived there, he was mistaken by the military academy for the new gardener, named Leo, and the academy officials assumed that August Wennerström would be that new gardener. In 1913, he found a job and a nickname that he would keep for the rest of his life - Leo.

August Wennerström was head of garden maintenance at the academy, until his retirement, in 1941. He also spoke frequently at the Academy, and elsewhere in the region, and around the country, especially in Swedish Methodist churches, about his experiences on the TITANIC. On Wednesday, November 22, 1950, August Wennerström died, at the age of 66. He was buried in the Masonic Cemetery in Culver, Indiana.

THE LONGFORD-GIRLS

At the beginning of the last century, many young people in Europe and especially in Ireland dreamed of the so-called "New World" and it brought four young women from the peaceful County Longford in central Ireland together and on board of the brand-new RMS TITANIC.

Hoping for a better life in America, sisters Kate (18) and Margaret Murphy (25), as well as Kate Mullin (21) and 17-year-old Kate Gilnagh, the youngest, boarded the TITANIC.

The eldest of this group, Margaret Murphy, had lived in the USA for several years before returning home in 1911 to care for her seriously ill father, who died on Wednesday, June 28, 1911.

On her return to Ireland, she had met Matthew O'Reilly from nearby Cortober, County Cavan, who, like her, had emigrated to America around 1905 and settled in New York before returning home to visit his family in Ireland.

The two fell in love and proposed to each other on the shores of nearby Lough Gowna. They planned to marry and settle down together in the USA, but Matthew was forced to return to New York earlier than planned. After his return to New York, he took residence with a sister and worked as a mortician. He was also sexton at St. Andrew's Church in the city.

In August 1911, John Kiernan, also from County Longford, aged 26, had returned for a home visit. When it was time for John and his younger brother Phillip (22) and their 19-year-old second cousin Thomas McCormack to leave Ireland, Margaret Murphy decided to join them in order to be with her fiancé as soon as possible. Her younger sister Kate had also decided to come along.

Margaret had promised her mother that she would stay in Ireland until her fiancé Matthew O'Reilly was settled and financially secure in New York, but her longing for Matthew was stronger. Her brother John had even wanted to forbid her to go to the USA.

In the meantime, the two Murphy sisters had secretly made plans to leave at the same time as the Kiernan brothers and their cousin and turn their backs on Ireland. For weeks, they secretly packed their luggage in a barn so that they would have it ready to hand when the time came.

Initially, they wanted to stay with their brother Patrick in Philadelphia and then build a new life for themselves in the USA, just as their sister Annie had done in Brooklyn.

On Thursday, April 11, 1912, Margaret and Kate Murphy boarded the TITANIC in Queeenstown as third-class passengers. They had purchased a joint ticket with the ticket number 367230 at a price of £15.10s.

On board the TITANIC, the sisters shared cabin 161 on E deck with Kate Gilnagh and Kate Mullin. By then they had become good friends.

Kate Gilnagh was on her way to visit her sister Mary "Mollie" who had already immigrated to America on Tuesday, April 9, 1911 aboard the LAURENTIC and was working in Manhattan and now wanted to catch up with her younger sister.

Kate Mullin was the youngest of nine children and had grown up in a Catholic household. Like Kate Gilnagh, she was on her way to join one of her sisters who had settled down in New York.

The four women were not the only ones on board the TITANIC from County Longford in central Ireland. As mentioned, John and Phillip Kiernan and their cousin Thomas McCormack also came from Longford. As well as James Farell (aged 26), the McCoy siblings (Agnes, Alice and Bernard) and Ellen Corr.

The McCoy siblings and Ellen Corr survived the sinking of the TITANIC, which is remarkable considering the high number of victims in third class.

On board the TITANIC, there was an excited, joyful atmosphere among the emigrants as the ship made its way to New York.

The friends thoroughly enjoyed their days on board the ship and could not wait to start a new life in America and escape poverty in Ireland.

On Sunday, April 14, 1912, the four of them and other passengers had a party in the third-class common rooms, during which a rat crawled across the floor and caused a commotion among those present.

The young women had just gone to bed when a man they had met on board knocked on their door and told them to get up because something was wrong with the ship.

For some time, they waited in vain with the men from Longford for further instructions. When the water reached the steerage, unlike many other third-class passengers, they no longer hesitated and tried to make their way to the boat deck.

But their way up was abruptly halted because, as in many other places on the ship, locked iron bars blocked access to the top. There were also scuffles between some third-class men and crew members who were determined to keep the steerage passengers down.

And now the four friends stood behind one of the many iron bars and tried to persuade a sailor to open it. But he refused.

James Farrell had finally had enough and shouted to the sailor in a powerful voice: "*For God's sake, open the gate and let these girls through!*"

The resolute and harsh tone broke the sailor's resistance so that he finally opened the gate and let the people through.

James Farrell thus became the savior of the four women and is still held in honor by the descendants of the rescued girls.

Margaret Murphy also told the "Irish Independent" on May 9, 1912 how the passengers were held back:

"A group of men were trying to get to a higher deck and were fighting with the sailors, hitting and scuffling and swearing. Women and some children were there, praying and crying. Then the sailors closed the hatches leading to third class, saying they wanted to keep the air down there so the ship could stay up longer."[36]

In her hurry, Katie Gilnagh lost sight of her friends and got lost on the second-class promenade deck. When she had walked the promenade deck in both directions, Katie finally spotted a man leaning over the railing, staring lost in thought into the dark night. She approached the man and asked him how to get to the boat deck. The man replied that he would show her the shortest way and without further ado let her climb onto his shoulders and lifted her straight up to the next deck up.

On the boat deck, lifeboat number 16 was about to be launched, so Katie immediately ran off without paying any attention to the other boats. When she finally arrived, she was turned back by a sailor. In her distress, Katie shouted that she had to get to her sister, who was already on board. The sailor looked a little confused for a moment, but then granted Katie access and unlocked the hawsers to lower the boat. There, Katie reunited with her friends, whom she had previously lost in the chaos. Her lifeboat number 16 was launched shortly after boat number 14.

---

[36]Margaret Murphy- The Irish Independent- May 9, 1912

It was 1:35 a.m. when their boat left the sinking TITANIC under the command of Officer in Charge Joseph Henry Bailey, assisted by the two seamen James Forward and Ernest Edward Archer. In the boat was another from Longford, Thomas McCormack, who later said that he had been taken out of the water and lifted into the boat by the Murphy sisters. His cousins, the Kiernan brothers, did not survive the night.

Their lifesaver James Farrell went down with the TITANIC. The last time he was seen, he was kneeling next to his suitcase praying the rosary. Of the twelve young people who came from Longford, nine survived the sinking of the TITANIC and thus fared much better than the Addergoole 14, of whom only three survived the sinking.

The Carpathia with the TITANIC survivors on board is awaited by a large crowd in New York © Library of Congress

The two Murphy sisters were greeted by their overjoyed siblings when the CARPATHIA arrived, and another face in the crowd was Matthew O'Reilly. He had known nothing of Margaret's intention to return to the USA and marry him. He had only become aware when he saw the names of Margaret and her sister Kate on a list of survivors:

„He was at the pier to meet them when they came off the Carpathia and from that night laid siege to the heart of the fair colleen. "[37]

Like many other survivors, the two Murphy sisters were taken to St. Vincent Hospital in New York to recover.

The survivors of the TITANIC at their arrival in New York © Library of Congress

---

[37] Quote: The Evening World, July 16, 1913

After their recovery, Margaret and Kate accompanied Matthew O'Reilly and his sister to their home at 17 City Hall Place in New York. A portrait of the two surviving sisters was taken there and printed in "The Advocate", an Irish-American newspaper, on Saturday, April 27, 1912.

Margaret subsequently gave several interviews in which she stated, among other things:

„Perhaps the most interesting story was that told by Margaret Murphy, a typical colleen beauty, with even features, rosy cheeks and pure Irish blue eyes, who left her home in Fostra, County Longford without even the knowledge of her parents and relatives, on board the Titanic, with the intention of marrying here John Kiernan, a neighbour, who was in her party. When the critical moment of shipwreck came Kiernan gave up his life for her when he surrended his lifebelt to her and saw her safely in a boat. When he heard the Titanic was doomed, we all left our berths and rushed on deck. I saw boat after boat loaded with passengers while I stood trembling at the side of Mr. Kiernan. He tried to cheer me, and the truth of the matter is I never thought for a moment that the steamship was going down. When both of us realised that it was, Mr. Kiernan took a lifebelt off himself and assisted me in one of the last lifeboats to leave the steamship. We kissed each other goodbye and he promised to see me soon. "[38]

Margaret gave another interview to the "Altoona Times" in which she described how she came aboard the TITANIC, which appeared on Thursday, May 2, 1912:

---

[38] Source: The Sun (Baltimore), April 29, 1912

„The night before the little group in our village was to leave to go aboard the Titanic, together with several other young women and men, I slipped away from my home, carrying all the clothes I could, and went to the Kiernan home, where a farewell party was being held. At that time, I had promised to wait at home, until Mr. Kiernan would come to this country and make a place. Then I was going to join him. But the thoughts of being separeted from him was too much for me and I decided to run away from home.

At the Kiernan home I was received kindly, as we were all neighbours. At the first opportunity I told Mr. Kiernan of my purpose. He reluctantly agreed. He was twenty-five and I am nineteen."[39]

If you read through these interviews, you inevitably get the impression that Margaret and John Kiernan were lovers who wanted to run away with TITANIC. This was completely untrue and it seems that the newspapers added a few things to make the story more exciting. Even the age information shows that the press had cheated, because she was not 19 years old, but already 25 years old...

In the months that followed, Maggie, who had meanwhile reported the New York press for libel, was forced to turn to the newspapers to clarify the relationship between her and John Kiernan:

„Miss Maggie J. Murphy at present of Wms`Bridge, New York, and late of Fostra, Aughnacliffe, one of the Irish girls saved from the Titanic, writes to us to ask us to correct a

---

[39] Interview with Margaret Murphy, Altoona Times, May 2, 1912

statement made in the Yellow (tabloid) press in New York to the effect that on her trip on the ill-fated ship she was eloping with John Kiernan, one of the two brothers drowned in the disaster.

As a modest, respectable Irish girl, Miss Murphy rightly complains of the cruelty and injustice both to her and the poor young fellow who drowned of the typical American media invention. We have much pleasure in giving her flat contradiction and assuring her that the people at home did not believe any such Yankee yarn.[40]

Just over a year later, in July 1913, Margaret and Matthew were married, and the New York media reported on the wedding:

TITANIC SURVIVOR WED

„Margaret Murphy Bride of Church Sexton, with sister, Also survivor, as Bridesmaid Margaret Murphy, one of the survivors of the Titanic disaster, was married in St. Andrew`s Church, in Duane Street, yesterday, with her sister Katherine, also a Titanic survivor, as her bridemaid. She became of the bride of Matthew O`Reilly, sexton of St. Andrews.

A wooing which began when O`Reilly met Miss Murphy on the night the steamship Carpathia arrived with those whose lives were saved in the wreck, resulted in the wedding yesterday. The Rev Patrick Masterson, cousin of O`Reilly, performed the ceremony and was the celebrant at a nuptial mass.

---

[40] Source: Unidentified newspaper, August 3, 1912

Many friends of the couple attended the wedding. A wedding breakfast was served in O'Reilly's old home, No.17 City Hall place, following the ceremony. Hundreds of persons followed the bridal party to one of the Chelsea piers, where they boarded the steamship Coronia, bound for Europe. They will pass three months in County Cavan, Ireland, of which they are both natives. "[41]

Again, it is interesting that the impression is given that Margaret and Matthew only met after the arrival of the CARPATHIA, which is definitely not true, because the two were already engaged to each other beforehand and Margaret was only on board the TITANIC to get faster to Matthew to marry him in America.

Margaret and Matthew spent their honeymoon in Ireland to visit Margaret's family, whom she had left overnight over a year earlier. Overjoyed, she embraced the family again.

Margaret and Matthew settled in Manhattan and had three children: Margaret (1917-1959), Anna Marie (1919-2004) and Matthew (1921-1998).

They had a very happy marriage, but unfortunately their time together was short, as Matthew was diagnosed with cancer and died on Saturday, April 15, 1939, the 27th anniversary of the TTTANIC disaster.

Margaret never remarried and rarely spoke about TITANIC during her lifetime.

---

[41] Quote: New York Press, July 17, 1913

On Sunday, September 29, 1957, Margaret Murphy O'Reilly died at the age of 70 while visiting her daughter Anna in Slate Hill, Orange, New York. She was buried at Calvary Cemetery in Queens, New York.

Her younger sister Kate, like her sister, married on July 17, 1913 to Michael Guilfoyle, whose brother Denis had married Kate's other sister Anna the year before; the two had met through their respective siblings.

Her husband had emigrated to the USA in November 1907 on the CELTIC of the White Star Line and was a policeman in Brooklyn and later an inspector with the US Customs Service.

Kate and Michael settled in New York and had three children: Marie Josephine (born June 2, 1914), Michael Joseph (born August 8, 1916) and Rita Catherine (born January 16, 1919). The family lived in Brooklyn until the 1940s.

In December 1919, Kate, who never returned to Ireland herself, sent her three-year-old son Michael to the old country to spend time with Kate's mother. The visit turned into several years and little Michael and his mother were not reunited until May 1924.

In later years, Kate never wanted to talk about the TITANIC disaster, and she outlived her older sister Margaret by several years.

Kate and her husband Michael spent the last years of their lives at their home in Swan Lake, where Michael died on Tuesday, October 2, 1962 after a long illness.

Kate lived just outlived him by under six years and died on Tuesday, September 24, 1968, while visiting relatives in Brooklyn. She was buried with her husband at St. Peter's Cemetery in Sullivan, New York, just a few weeks before her 75th birthday (although the obituary said she was 68).

After her arrival in New York, Kate Mullin first moved in with her sister Mrs. Murray at 231 East 50th Street in New York. After some time, she finally found a job as a domestic servant in New York.

She later described her experiences on the TITANIC to her father, telling him that her boat was loaded with over 50 people and that the screams of the people left on board would haunt her.

On Sunday, January 2, 1916, she married the laborer Martin Kearns in Mannhattan and had four children with him: Margaret "Peggy (born 1918), Mary (born 1919), Eileen (born 1922) and John Thomas (born 1925).

The family lived in the Bronx, New York, for two decades before moving to Queens, New York, where they lived in the 1940s and Martin Kearns worked on the city's docks.

Kate was never to see her old home in Ireland again.

Kate suffered a heavy blow in 1944 when her only son John died at the age of 19 in the sinking of a troopship. This loss hit her very hard.

She mostly kept quiet about her traumatic experiences on the TITANIC. However, on a few occasions she spoke about it with her family or the local media. She was interviewed again on the 50th anniversary of the sinking, and in this interview, she thanked God for her survival, but emphasized that she did not want to be reminded of this terrible event.

On Sunday, November 1, 1970, Kate Mullin Kearns died in Queens at the age of 80. After a mass at St. Sebastian's Roman Catholic Church, she was buried at St. Raymond's Cemetery in the Bronx. Incidentally, her obituary made no reference to her connection with TITANIC.

Kate Gilnagh was embraced by her overjoyed sister Mollie on her arrival in New York.

To document to her anxious family in Ireland that Kate had survived the sinking of the TITANIC and was safe, the two sisters had a photograph taken of themselves and sent to their parents in Ireland. Only when they held the photo in their hands could they believe that their daughter was well and had arrived safely at her sister's home.

Kate settled in America very quickly, also with the help of her sister, and very soon she met and fell in love with her later husband John Joseph Manning and they married in 1917.

Their very happy marriage produced four children: John (born in 1919), Thomas (born in 1923), Catherine (born in 1924) and Joseph Eugene (born in 1927).

The family initially lived in Boston before moving to Queens, New York.

On Tuesday, April 19, 1955, John Manning died and Kate was left a grieving widow and did not remarry.

In the years that followed, she became a member of the Titanic Enthusiasts of America, which later became the Titanic Historical Society, co-founded by Edward Kamuda in 1963. She appeared in two television programs, "To Tell the Truth and the "Steve Allen Show. In 1953, her experiences on the TITANIC appeared in Life magazine.

She also shared her memories with Walter Lord when he wrote the TITANIC bible "A Night to Remember", which also recounted parts of her experiences on that terrible night.

On Monday, March 1, 1971, Kate Gilnagh Manning died at the age of 76 in Long Island City, New York, and was buried with her husband at Woodside Cemetery in Queens, New York.

THE STORY OF KATE MULLIN AND KATE MURPHY WAS ALSO USED IN A MODIFIED FORM IN THE SUCCESSFUL BROADWAY MUSICAL "TITANIC" BY PETER STONE AND MAURY YESTON.

THE DRAMA OF THE ASPLUND FAMILY

Another dramatic story is the story of the seven-member Asplund family. It shows how difficult it was to survive the sinking of the TITANIC as a third-class family with several members.

The parents Carl Oscar Vilhelm Gustafsson Asplund (aged 40) and Selma Augusta Emilia Asplund (née Johansson, aged 38) came from Sweden and had emigrated to America in 1894, settling in Worcester, Massachusetts.

Their children Filip Oscar (born Monday, December 12, 1898), Clarence Gustaf Hugo (born Wednesday, September 17, 1902) and the twins Lillian Gertrud and Carl Edgar (born Sunday, October 21, 1906) were born there. This means, that their children were American citizens.

To settle the estate of Carl Oscar's father after his death and to care for his mother, the family returned to Sweden in 1907 and lived in Alseda, where they had their fifth child Edvin Roij Felix (born Friday, March 19, 1909).

In 1912, Carl Oscar had the opportunity to return to his former position as a worker at the Spencer Wire Works in Worcester. He did not want to miss this opportunity and so the decision was made to return home to America.

In April 1912, the family of seven made their way from Sweden to Southampton to board the brand-new TITANIC on April 10, 1912. The family had ticket number 347077 and paid £31 7s for the ticket.

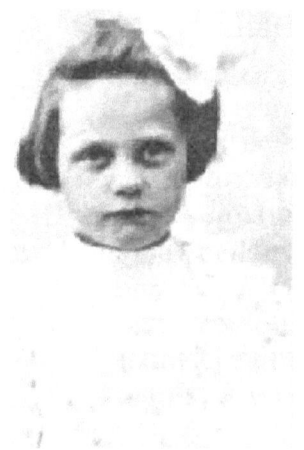

Lillian Asplund as a young girl © public domain

Like many third-class families, the Asplunds spent their days on board trying to find their way around the huge ocean liner.

But they enjoyed the days very much, as the food was delicious and the accommodation in third class was far more luxurious than on other ships of the time.

Shortly after the TITANIC struck the iceberg, the family was woken by the stewards and after a while they found themselves in a large crowd on the boat deck. Their luck was no doubt that, unlike many steerage passengers, their years in America had given them very good English language skills.

Their fate was decided on the starboard side of the sinking ship. At around 1:35 a.m., when the TITANIC only had 45 minutes left, lifeboat number 15 was launched with 67 people on board.

It was already at the deck level when Selma Asplund, with her youngest child Felix in her arms, jumped into the boat at the very last second.

The TITANIC leaving the port of Southampton © Authors collection

Her husband Carl realized the dramatic situation, grabbed little Lillian and threw her to his wife into the lifeboat. However, it was already too late to get the other children safely into the lifeboat, as it was already halfway to the surface.

Selma Asplund only saw Carl and the other children disappear into the crowd and assumed that they had also managed to get into a lifeboat.

It was only on board the CARPATHIA that it emerged that Carl Asplund and the three other young sons had not survived the sinking of the TITANIC. Carl Asplund's body was later recovered by the MACKAY-BENNETT and buried sometime later in the Swedish Cemetery in Worcester, Massachusetts. The three remaining children remained missing forever.

After being rescued by the CARPATHIA, mother Selma Asplund and her two children Lillian and Felix were taken to St. Vincent Hospital in New York City. After they were able to leave the hospital, they returned to Worcester as planned, where they lived in Selma Asplund's sister's house at 151 Vernon Street. The family had lost all their belongings and money when the luxury liner sank.

To support the family financially, the city of Worcester organized a very successful charity event that raised a total of almost 2.000 dollars for the Asplund family.

The money was put into a trust fund for the family. One of the trustees was the Mayor of the City of Worcester, David F. O'Conell. The interest from this fund was paid out to the family as needed.

In 1951, the family moved to Shrewsbury, Massachusetts.

Selma Asplund never got over the terrible tragedy that had robbed her of her husband and three of her children. She never spoke about the TITANIC again. She died on the 52nd anniversary of the sinking, on Wednesday, April 15, 1964 at the age of 90.

Her children Lillian and Felix remained unmarried and lived with her until her death.

Lillian and Felix rarely spoke about the TITANIC. In one of their rare interviews, Lillian recalled how she was smuggled into a lifeboat through a window on the first-class promenade deck, looking back at the sinking TITANIC. She said that for much of her life she was haunted by the faces of her father and three brothers who went down with the TITANIC. She also remembered her father holding her twin brother Carl in his arms and her older brothers standing on either side of the railing.

Felix Asplund died on Tuesday, March 1, 1983 at the age of 73. His older sister Lillian was the last of the survivors who lived the longest to remember the sinking of the TITANIC. She died on Saturday, May 6, 2006, six months before her 100th birthday.

THE STORY OF FRANKIE GOLDSMITH

At the beginning of 1912, there was still a great sadness in the Goldsmith house. The parents Frank and Emily and their nine-year-old son Frank John William, called Frankie, were mourning the death of six-year-old Albert John, called Bertie, who had died of diphtheria at the end of 1911.

Frankie had loved his little brother Bertie very much and was still very shocked and saddened by his early and sudden death.

A rare photo of the entire Goldsmith family © Library of Congress

His parents discussed what they should do now, as they felt very lonely in Strood, Kent in England, also because Emily's parents and six of her twelve siblings had already emigrated to America in 1910 and settled in Detroit, Michigan.

After a long discussion, they also decided to emigrate to Detroit and join Emily's family.

After extensive travel preparations, the family boarded the TITANIC in Southampton on April 10, 1912 as third-class passengers (ticket number 363291 at a price of £20, 10s, 6d).

Father Frank's tool bag, which he could certainly use as a toolmaker in America, also went on board the ship.

The family of three was accompanied by Thomas Theobald, a friend of Frank's, and Alfred Rush, the son of a family friend.

On Sunday, April 14, Albert Rush celebrated his 16th birthday.

On board the TITANIC, the Goldsmiths met and befriended many other British passengers, including: May Howard, Emily Badman, Rosa Abbott, Edward Lockyer and Edward Dorking.

For bright little Frankie, the huge TITANIC was an adventure playground and he spent his time on board playing with a group of English-speaking third-class boys who were all about his age: Willie Coutts (aged 9), Harold Goodwin (aged 10), William Johnston (aged 8),

Albert (aged 10) and George Rice (aged 8) as well as James (aged 10) and Walter van Billiard (aged 9).

The boys climbed up on the baggage cranes or went down into the boiler rooms to watch the stokers at work.

Frankie later remembered sticking their heads into a boiler room and watching the stokers at work, singing and banging their shovels to the beat of the music.

Of these adventurous and curious boys, only Frankie Goldsmith and Willie Coutts survived the sinking.

On the night of the sinking, the family was in their cabin; Frankie slept through the crash and was only woken up by his father.

Together with Thomas Theobald and Alfred Rush, the Goldsmiths made their way to the upper decks.

They made it to collapsible boat C, which was being loaded. A ring of crew members only let women and children through. Frankie remembered it very well:

"Mother and I were then let through the gate, and the man in charge of the crew seized Alfred Rush's arm to pull him through, for he must have realized that the young fellow was not much older than I was, and he was not very tall for his age, but Alfred had not hesitated. He snatched the sailor's arm out of his hand and said with his head held high, and I quote:

"No! I'm staying here with the men". He died a hero at the age of 16. "[42]

Thomas Theobald gave Emily his wedding ring and asked her if she would give it to his wife if he didn't survive.

"My father reached down, patted me on the shoulder and said, "Take care, Frankie, I'll see you later!" He didn't, and maybe he knew he wouldn't."[43]

His father Frank Goldsmith Sr, Thomas Theobald and Alfred Rush died in the sinking. Only Thomas Theobald's body was later recovered.

Little Frankie and his mother were among those rescued in Collapsible C. When the CARPATHIA sailed for New York, Emily placed her son in the care of surviving stoker Samuel Collins, who had survived in the infamous lifeboat number 1, which was cast off with only 12 people on board. He was to distract Frankie from the sinking.

Emily, meanwhile, was busy sewing clothes from blankets for women and children who had left the ship in nothing but nightgowns.

Samuel Collins took Frankie to meet his fellow stokers from the CARPATHIA, who offered to make Frankie an

---

[42] Source: Memories of a Titanic Survivor-Frankie Goldsmith, 1991
[43] Source; Memories of a Titanic Survivor-Frankie Goldsmith, 1991

honorary seaman by making him drink a mixture of water, vinegar and a whole raw egg.

Frankie proudly gulped down the mixture and from then on considered himself a member of the ship's crew. Frankie remembered Collins saying to him:

"Don't cry, Frankie, your father will probably be in New York before you!" [44]

After arriving in New York, Emily and Frankie were looked after by the Salvation Army, which organized their train journey to Detroit to see their relatives, who welcomed them with relief.

Emily kept in touch for many years with several survivors she had met, especially Rosa Abbott.

On Sunday, May 2, 1914, she married Harry Illman, a fellow countryman who had emigrated in 1913, was also from Strood and worked on the railroad. The couple had no children and later lived at 6190 Vermont Avenue in Detroit.

On Thursday, September 22, 1955, Emily died during a train ride in Ohio at the age of 75. Her husband Harry died on Friday, January 25, 1963 and they are buried together in Ashland Cemetery in Ashland, Ohio.

Growing up, Frankie held on to the hope that his father had survived. It was many months before he realized

---

[44] Source: Memories of a Titanic Survivor-Frankie Goldsmith, 1991

that his father was really dead. For years he said to himself:

"I think another ship must have picked him up, and one day he'll come through that door and say, "Hi Frankie!"[45]

When Frankie was growing up in Detroit, his house was near a baseball stadium. He later recalled that every time a home run was hit, the roar of the crowd reminded him of the sound of hundreds of people screaming for their lives in the water. This haunted him so much that he never took his own children to a baseball game.

Frankie went to school in Detroit and at the age of 17 worked as a stock clerk in a car factory. He later worked as a salesman for a dairy company for many years.

He also coached the girls' basketball team at Woodward Avenue Presbyterian Church, where he met his future wife Victoria Agnes Lawrence, who was from Michigan.

At first, they couldn't stand each other, but after a while they fell in love and married in 1926. They had three sons: James Richard (born 1927), Charles B. (born 1934) and Frank John (born 1936).

Every year in April, Frankie became very quiet because the memories of the TITANIC haunted him too much.

During World War II, he served as a civilian photographer for the US Army Air Corps. After the war,

---

[45] Source: Memories of a Titanic Survivor-Frankie Goldsmith, 1991

he and his family moved to Ashland, Ohio, where he opened a photography supply store near Mansfield.

In 1966, he was asked by the president of his Rotary Club to report on his experiences on the TITANIC.

Some of his very interesting and moving interviews can be found today on the Internet and in the archives of various television stations.

Frankie was very involved in the newly founded Titanic Historical Society and took part in several conventions in the 1970s, where he met other TITANIC survivors.

Since suffering his first stroke in 1970, his health has gone from bad to worse. He also developed very painful arthritis.

In April 1982, he was due to attend the Titanic Historical Society conference in Philadelphia and was already looking forward to it. But on Wednesday, January 27, 1982, at the age of 79, he succumbed to another stroke after staying up late that night watching the news.

Sometime earlier, he had written a book about his experiences on the TITANIC. This autobiography was published posthumously in 1991 by the Titanic Historical Society under the title "Memories of a Titanic Survivor". The famous author of "A night to remember", Walter Lord, wrote the foreword. It is the only book about the sinking written by a third-class passenger.

Frankie was cremated at his own request. On Thursday, April 15, 1982, 70 years after the sinking of the TITANIC, his ashes were scattered above the SOS position of the TITANIC in the North Atlantic.

Survivors Ruth Becker and Fourth Officer Joseph Boxhall were also scattered there.

His widow Victoria died on Thursday, September 30, 1993 at the age of 87 and is buried in Strickland Cemetery in Hayesville, Ashland, Ohio.

THE DRAMATIC RESCUE OF OLAUS ABELSETH

Born in Ålesund, Norway, 25-year-old Olaus Abelseth lived with his parents and his five siblings Inga, Hanna, Gina Jensine, Gurine and Hans as well as the foster daughter of the Olivie O. Tendfjordnes family and the maid Anne Olsdatter in Kleven, Örskog until 1902.

Life in Norway was hard and full of hardship, so Olaus and his brother Hans decided to follow the call of the New World and emigrate to America. They made the long journey overseas and settled in Hatton, North Dakota. There Olaus worked on various farms in the Red River Valley.

In 1908, Olaus established his own cattle ranch in Perkins County, South Dakota.

After a very difficult time on his farm, he decided to visit his relatives in Norway. In the late autumn of 1911, he traveled by steamship from New York to Glasgow in Scotland. From there he continued his journey to Scandinavia.

After a few months in his old homeland and with his family, he set off on his journey to Minneapolis, USA, in April 1912.

Five other Norwegians traveled with him: Adolf Humblen, Anna Salkjelsvik, Peter Søholt (Olaus' cousin), his brother-in-law Sigurd Hansen Moen, who was married to Olaus' sister Inge, and Karen Marie Abelseth, who despite having the same surname was not a relative of Olaus, but the daughter of one of Olaus' neighbors when he lived in Norway.

As Karen was only 16 years old, her father had asked Olaus to protect her during the trip to America.

The group of six sailed from Ålesund via Bergen to Newcastle before boarding the TITANIC in Southampton on April 10, 1912. Olaus Abelseth had ticket number 348122 and paid £7 13s for his ticket.

On board the ship, Olaus and Adolf Humblen shared a cabin towards the bow on F deck (G63), while his brother-in-law and cousin occupied cabin G73.

The days on board were also very peaceful for the six Norwegians and they enjoyed the comforts that third class also had to offer.

Olaus later reported about his experiences on board the TITANIC to the American inquiry to investigate the sinking of the ship. This inquiry had been hastily convened after the disaster in order to investigate the circumstances of the disaster. On Friday, May 3, 1912, Olaus also testified as a witness and was questioned by Senator William Alden Smith about his experiences:

"I went to bed about 10 o'clock Sunday night, and I think it was about 15 minutes to 12 when I woke up; and there was another man in the same room - two of us in the same room - and he said to me, "What is that?" I said, "I don't know, but we had better get up." So, we did get up and put our clothes

on, and we two went up on deck in the forward part of the ship. Then there was quite a lot of ice on the starboard part of the ship. They wanted us to go down again, and I saw one of the officers, and I said to him: "Is there any danger?" He said, "No." I was not satisfied with that, however, so I went down and told my brother-in-law and my cousin, who were in the same compartment there. They were not in the same room, but they were just a little way from where I was. I told them about what was happening, and I said they had better get up. Both of them got up and dressed, and we took our overcoats and put them on. We did not take any life belts with us. There was no water on the deck at that time. We walked to the hind part of the ship and got two Norwegian girls up. One was in my charge and one was in charge of the man who was in the same room with me. He was from the same town that I came from. The other one was just 16 years old, and her father told me to take care of her until we got to Minneapolis. The two girls were in a room in the hind part of the ship, in the steerage. We all went up on deck and stayed there. We walked over to the port side of the ship, and there were five of us standing, looking, and we thought we saw a light."[46]

This is a very interesting detail that Olaus Abelseth mentions here, and Senator William Alden Smith did not let it rest:

Senator Smith: *"On what deck were you standing?*

Olaus Abelseth: *"Not on the top deck, but on - I do not know what you call it, but it is the hind part, where the sitting room is; and then there is a kind of a little space in between, where they go up on deck. It was up on the boat deck, the place for the*

---

[46] Source: Olaus Abelseth's testimony at the American Inquiry ,Friday, May 3, 1912

steerage passengers on the deck. We were then on the port side there, and we looked out at this light. I said to my brother-in-law: "I can see it plain, now. It must be a light."

Senator Smith: *"How far away was it?*

Olaus Abelseth:*" I could not say, but it did not seem to be so very far. I thought I could see this mast light, the front mast light. That is what I thought I could see. A little while later there was one of the officers who came and said to be quiet, that there was a ship coming. That is all he said."*

Olaus was also questioned about whether any third class passengers were being held back:

"There were a lot of steerage people there that were getting on one of these cranes that they had on deck, that they used to lift things with. They can lift about two and a half tons, I believe. These steerage passengers were crawling along on this, over the railing, and away up to the boat deck. A lot of them were doing that. "

Senator Smith: *"They could not get up there in any other way?*

Olaus Abelseth: *"This gate was shut."*

Senator Smith: *"Was it locked?"*

Olaus Abelseth: *"I do not know whether it was locked, but it was shut so that they could not go that way. A while later these girls were standing there, and one of the officers came and hollered for all of the ladies to come up on the boat deck. The gate was opened and these two girls went up. We stayed a little while longer, and then they said, "Everybody." I do not know who that was, but I think it was some of the officers that said it. I could not say that, but it was somebody that said "everybody." We went up."*

Senator Smith: *"Do you think the passengers in the steerage and in the bow of the boat had an opportunity to get out and up on the decks, or were they held back?"*

Olaus Abelseth: *"Yes, I think they had an opportunity to get up."*

Senator Smith: *"There were no gates or doors locked, or anything that kept them down?"*

Olaus Abelseth: *"No, sir; not that I could see"*

Senator Smith: *"You said that a number of them climbed up one of these cranes?"*

Olaus Abelseth: *"That was on the top, on the deck; after they got on the deck. That was in order to get up on this boat deck."*

Senator Smith: *"Onto the top deck?"*

Olaus Abelseth: *"Onto the top deck; yes. But down where we were, in the rooms, I do not think there was anybody that held anybody back."*

Senator Smith: *"You were not under any restraint? You were permitted to go aboard the boats the same as other passengers?"*

Olaus Abelseth: *"Yes, sir."*

Senator Smith: *"Do you think the steerage passengers in your part of the ship all got out?"*

Olaus Abelseth: *"I could not say that for sure; but I think the most of them got out."*[47]

When Olaus finally made it onto the boat deck, he tried his luck on the port side together with his brother-in-law and his cousin, but found that there were only two boats left. The men then went over to the starboard side. There, one of the officers came by and asked if there were any sailors, but as his brother-in-law and cousin asked him to stay with them, Olaus did not come forward, even though he had been a fisherman for six years.

"Then we stayed there, and we were just standing still there. We did not talk very much. Just a little way from us I saw there was an old couple standing there on the deck, and I heard this man say to the lady, "Go into the lifeboat and get saved." He put his hand on her shoulder and I think he said: "Please get into the lifeboat and get saved." She replied: "No; let me stay with you." I could not say who it was, but I saw that he was an old man. I did not pay much attention to him, because I did not know him."

HERE, OLAUS ABELTSETH SEEMS ALMOST CERTAIN TO HAVE SEEN THE LEGENDARY COUPLE IDA AND ISIDOR STRAUS, WHO WENT DOWN TOGETHER WITH THE TITANIC.

---

[47] Source: Olaus Abelseth's testimony at the American Inquiry ,Friday, May 3, 1912

"I was standing there, and I asked my brother-in-law if he could swim and he said no. I asked my cousin if he could swim and he said no. So we could see the water coming up, the bow of the ship was going down, and there was a kind of an explosion. We could hear the popping and cracking, and the deck raised up and got so steep that the people could not stand on their feet on the deck. So they fell down and slid on the deck into the water right on the ship. Then we hung onto a rope in one of the davits. We were pretty far back at the top deck. My brother-in-law said to me, "We had better jump off or the suction will take us down." I said, "No. We won't jump yet. We ain't got much show anyhow, so we might as well stay as long as we can." So he stated again, "We must jump off.," But I said, "No; not yet." So, then, it was only about 5 feet down to the water when we jumped off. It was not much of a jump. Before that we could see the people were jumping over. There was water coming onto the deck, and they were jumping over, then, out in the water. My brother-in-law took my hand just as we jumped off; and my cousin jumped at the same time. When we came into the water, I think it was from the suction - or anyway we went under, and I swallowed some water. I got a rope tangled around me, and I let loose of my brother-in-law's hand to get away from the rope. I thought then, "I am a goner." That is what I thought when I got tangled up in this rope. But I came on top again, and I was trying to swim, and there was a man - lots of them were floating around - and he got me on the neck like that [illustrating] and pressed me under, trying to get on top of me. I said to him, "Let go." Of course, he did not pay any attention to that, but I got away from him. Then there was another man, and he hung on to me for a while, but he let go. Then I swam; I could not say, but it must have been about 15 or 20 minutes. It could not have been over that. Then I saw something dark ahead of me. I did not know what it was, but I swam toward that, and it was one of

those collapsible boats. When we jumped off of the ship, we had life preservers on. There was no suction from the ship at all. I was lying still, and I thought "I will try to see if I can float on the life belt without help from swimming," and I floated easily on the life belt. When I got on this raft or collapsible boat, they did not try to push me off and they did not do anything for me to get on. All they said when I got on there was, "Don't capsize the boat." So, I hung onto the raft for a little while before I got on. Some of them were trying to get up on their feet. They were sitting down or lying down on the raft. Some of them fell into the water again. Some of them were frozen; and there were two dead, that they threw overboard. I got on this raft or collapsible boat and raised up, and then I was continually moving my arms and swinging them around to keep warm. [48]

Olaus Abelseth survived this terrible night and was one of the lucky ones to reach the deck of the CARPATHIA the morning after the sinking.

OF THE ORIGINAL GROUP OF SIX, ONLY ANNA SALKJELSVIK, KAREN MARIE ABELSETH AND OLAUS ABELSETH SURVIVED THE SINKING OF THE TITANIC.

There he was immediately given a warm blanket. He then went into the dining room for a schnapps and hot coffee. He slept on board the CARPATHIA the whole time in the same clothes he had worn during the night in the flooded boat.

---

[48] Source: Olaus Abelseth's testimony at the American Inquiry ,Friday, May 3, 1912

After his arrival in New York, he stayed in St. Vincent Hospital for a few days because the hypothermia he had suffered in the icy water was getting to him. After giving his testimony to the American Inquiry, he finally left for Minneapolis.

In 1912 and 1913, he traveled to Canada, Indianapolis and Montana before returning to his farm in South Dakota.

In July 1915, he married Anna Grinde in South Dakota. She was his first wife, while he was her second husband.

Olaus worked on his farm for another 30 years and had four children with Anna. However, their second son died at the age of 3½, the other children were named George, Helen and Mae.

In 1946 he retired to Reeder, North Dakota. Two years later they moved to Tacoma, Washington and finally to Whetting, North Dakota in 1960 before settling in Hettinger, Adams Co, North Dakota.

His wife Anna celebrated her 100th birthday in 1977 and died in August 1978.

Olaus Abelseth died on Thursday, December 4, 1980, at the age of 94, making him the second longest living male survivor of the TITANIC tragedy. He was buried in Glendo Cemetery in Ralph, South Dakota.

THE ADVENTUROUS JOURNEY OF TWO SIBLINGS ON BOARD THE TITANIC

After leaving the port of Southampton, the TITANIC made her way to the French port of Cherbourg, where she arrived in the early evening of April 10, 1912.

As the TITANIC was unable to berth in Cherbourg due to its enormous size, the 274 passengers (142 first class, 30 second class and 102 third class) were taken on board by the two tenders of the White Star Line, TRAFFIC and NOMADIC.

The NOMADIC just after the turn of the century. © public domain

The NOMADIC in Belfast in 2024 © Private photo Norbert Zimmermann

There, two underage Lebanese siblings boarded the brand-new luxury liner. They were 11-year-old Ilyās Nīqūla Yārid and his 13-year-old sister Jamīlah Nīqūla Yārid.

Their family had gradually emigrated from Lebanon to the USA since 1904 and the two youngsters were the last family members to embark on the journey to the New World together with their father Nīqūla Yārid to join the rest of the family in Jacksonville, Florida.

In March 1912, the three had left their village in Lebanon to travel to Beirut. From there they traveled on to Marseille, where they bought a ticket for the maiden voyage of the TITANIC.

From Marseille, they traveled to Cherbourg to board the TITANIC.

However, they were in for a bad surprise, as Nīqūla Yārid was not allowed to board the ship due to an infectious eye infection and failed the obligatory medical examination.

However, his two underage children passed the examination and were allowed on board and after a short discussion, it was decided that the two siblings should embark on the long journey alone, while their father would stay in France and join them later.

So Jamīlah and Iyās Nīqūla Yārid boarded the TITANIC as third-class passengers (ticket number 2651, cost: £11, 4s, and 10 d). As neither spoke English, they were probably reliant on meeting and joining friendly compatriots on board the luxury liner.

The days on board the new ship were pleasant and calm and there were no signs of a disaster. The two siblings had quickly made friends in the large Lebanese community on board the TITANIC (the numbers vary from 93 to 125 Lebanese on board) and were looking forward to seeing their family again in the USA and hoped that their father would be able to join them as soon as possible.

When the TITANIC had the fatal collision with the iceberg at 23:40 on Sunday, the two siblings were already in bed.

Like many passengers in steerage, they were awakened by a violent bump and wondered about the loud noises they heard outside their cabin shortly afterwards as many excited passengers came out of their cabins wondering what had just happened and what the violent bump that had woken some of them was all about.

Jamīlah then asked her brother to investigate, but Ilyās showed no interest in leaving his warm bed, but his sister, two years older, prevailed and the two of them left their cabin and joined a larger group of steerage passengers on their arduous journey to the boat deck.

When they got there, Jamīlah remembered the 500 dollars her father had given them for their trip, so they made their way back to their cabin.

When they arrived at their cabin, however, they realized that the corridor was already filled with water and they could no longer open the door to their cabin.

They did the only right thing and decided that their lives were more important to them than the 500 dollars in their cabin, so they made their way back to the boat deck as fast as possible.

Once there, they were lucky enough to get into a lifeboat that had just been launched.

It is not known which lifeboat the two young Lebanese got into, but they survived the sinking of the TITANIC. This was an extra birthday present for Jamīlah, as April 15, 1912 was her 14th birthday.

On their arrival in New York, Jamīlah and Ilyās were met by their overjoyed older brother Isaac (1894-1985), who took them to his home in Nova Scotia, where they spent several months recovering from their traumatic experience.

It was in July 1912 that their father also arrived in the USA and the family was reunited and settled in Jacksonville as planned.

To make it easier for the two siblings to settle in their new home, he changed the family name from Yārid to Garrett and their first names were also changed from Jamīlah to Amelia and from Ilyās to Louis Nicholas.

On Sunday, December 13, 1914, Amelia married Isaac Abdallah Isaac, a Lebanese immigrant who was three years her elder and had already immigrated to the USA in 1905.

The couple had seven children together - four daughters and three sons. Her husband Isaac owned a grocery store and in later years acquired some real estate as an investment and worked as an oil supplier.

He died on Sunday, September 20, 1942 and Amelia never remarried and remained in Jacksonville for the rest of her life.

She became a local TITANIC celebrity over the years and was often asked to speak to school classes or give newspaper interviews. In 1953, she attended a screening of the Clifton Webb and Barbara Stanwyk movie "TITANIC" held in her honor at the Florida Theatre.

On Sunday, March 8, 1970, Amelia, formerly Jamīlah, died at the age of 71 and was laid to rest at Evergreen Cemetery in Jacksonville.

Her younger brother Louis initially worked for his older brother Isaac and lived with him in his house.

On Friday, February 5, 1926, he married his brother's sister-in-law Elizabeth Shedise, four years older, who was also a Lebanese immigrant who had come to the USA in 1900. The couple's first child, an unnamed son, was born on Saturday, April 2, 1927, but died the same day. Their son Kenneth was born two years later.

The small family continued to live in Jacksonville where Louis earned a living as a grocer. In later years he became a Jehovah's Witness and in the late 1940s traveled by plane back to his old home in Lebanon.

Unlike his older sister, he rarely spoke about his experiences on the TITANIC, and when he did, he became very emotional and often broke down in tears.

It hit him hard when his beloved sister Amelia died in 1970 and eleven years later, on Sunday, May 31, 1981, Louis, formerly Ilyās, died at the age of 81 in Tucker, Georgia, while visiting his son Kenneth, who had moved there with his wife Ann in 1973. Like his sister, he was buried in Evergreen Cemetery in Jacksonville.

THE SAD STORY OF ROSA ABBOTT

A year before the TITANIC set off on its fateful final voyage, the life of the then 38-year-old Rosa (Rhoda) Abbott had changed radically.

Her husband Stanton Abbott, who was a well-known heavyweight boxer and sports promoter in Providence (Rhode Island) at that time, had divorced her after 18 years of marriage and, almost penniless, she was forced to move into a small apartment with her two sons Eugene (aged 13) and Rossmore (aged 15), where she had to earn a living by sewing.

In August 1911, the need had become so great that she left the USA with her sons on the OLYMPIC and moved to live with her brother and mother in St. Albans in the English county of Hertfordshire.

But the two teenagers, who were born and grew up in America, quickly became homesick for their friends and their familiar surroundings in the USA and insisted that their mother should return to America.

The two boys were eventually able to persuade their mother and she organized their return trip to the USA with the help of the Salvation Army's emigration department.

Like many others, the Abbotts were supposed to travel on the PHILADELPHIA, but due to the nationwide coal miners' strike, the ship was stranded in Southampton.

So, they were transferred to the TITANIC and left Southampton on Wednesday, April 10, 1912 (ticket number CA2673).

The now 16-year-old Rossmore had written to his friends at Oxford Street School in Providence that he would come home.

On the night of the disaster, Rosa Abbott slept through the collision in her cabin, which was more than three cabin blocks away from the damage to the TITANIC. There the fateful collision with the iceberg was perceived only as a slight tremor, if it was noticed at all.

Shortly after midnight on Monday, April 15, 1912, a steward suddenly banged on her cabin door and demanded that Rosa, startled from her sleep, put on her life jacket.

After picking up her two sons, she waited desperate for help with the two teenagers at the foot of the stairs on E deck.

However, when no one attended to the steerage passengers waiting for instructions, the three of them made their own way to the boat deck.

Unfortunately for them, the Abbotts arrived on the port side of the deck of the TITANIC, which was already noticeably sinking.

There, second officer Charles Herbert Lightoller interpreted the captain's order "Women and children first" so strictly that he only allowed women and children (girls but no boys) into the lifeboats.

His colleague on the starboard side, first officer William McMaster Murdoch, also followed the order, but also allowed men and boys to board the boats when there were no more women and children nearby.

He preferred to fill the boats to the limit rather than to sail them half-empty. In this way, Murdoch saved the lives of countless men and boys.

The Abbott boys were not allowed through the guarded barrier on the well deck because, as 14- and 16-year-old teenagers, they were already men in the eyes of the officers.

One officer told Rosa that she could go to the boats, but only without her two sons. This was absolutely out of the question for Rosa and so she remained on board the TITANIC with very little chance of being rescued.

In the meantime, the well deck filled up with more and more third-class passengers coming out of the staircases onto the boat deck, only to realize that most of the lifeboats had already left the sinking ship.

Sensing that they would almost certainly not survive the night, 14-year-old Eugene fell on his knees and began praying for his mother's life. A heartbreaking scene!

When the bridge of the TITANIC sank into the icy North Atlantic and the stern of the ship was already rising noticeably, there was only one boat left to launch - Collapsible A.

The collapsible boat was fastened to the roof of the officers' quarters and all available hands were desperately struggling to heave the boat off the roof and into the wellin davits.

The steward, Edward Brown, had climbed into the boat and shouted that the ropes would have to be cut at the moment the ship sank into the deep. At just that moment, a huge wave of water washed the collapsible boat and the remaining passengers into the freezing ocean.

Rosa, who was standing nearby, clutched her sons' hands in deep despair as they were swept off the deck. She tried to hold them tight, but they slipped from her grasp.

Before her eyes, first Eugene and then Rossmore sank into the sea.

Gasping for air, Rosa fought her way through the crowds of people wriggling around her in the freezing water, tugging at her clothes and trying to pull herself up by her body.

She flailed her arms wildly as she searched for her sons among the wreckage and debris of the sunken luxury liner scattered in the sea, gasping and gasping for breath as she called out their names over and over again.

But it was hopeless. Her two sons had gone down with the ship.

After some time, she was pulled by strong hands into collapsible boat A, to which around 30 men were clinging at the time. They stood in ankle-deep ice water for hours, waiting for help.

By the end of the night, only twelve or 13 of the original 30 people were left, and the only woman among them was Rosa Abbott!

When the boat was already very low in the water shortly before sunrise, the people remaining in the boat saw another lifeboat heading in their direction under sail.

They screamed at the top of their lungs to draw attention to their more than dramatic plight and lifeboat number 14, under the command of Officer Harold Lowe, finally got all the passengers from the collapsible boat safely into his boat.

He then opened the onboard valves of the collapsible boat and cut the lines. The boat drifted away with three dead bodies on board, their faces covered with life jackets. On Friday, May 3, 1912, Collapsible Boat A was finally discovered by the OLYMPIC and the bodies were buried at sea.

Rosa could hardly remember the transfer in Lowe's lifeboat, but the stoker Thomas Threlfall stated that he held her in his arms until she was taken on board the CARPATHIA.

There she was given a makeshift bed which she hardly left in the following days.

She was understandably completely traumatized and the only contact she had was with Amy Stanley, whose cabin on the TITANIC had been very close to hers and who had known her two sons.

When Rosa talked to her about her sons and her life with them, Rose almost believed that the two boys could still be alive.

As she listened, Amy combed her hair calmly and gently, removing a stubborn piece of cork that had become entangled in Rosa's long, dark hair.

Amy Stanley later remembered it vividly:

"We were very close we were on the Titanic together. And her stateroom had been near mine. I was the only one that she could talk to about her sons because I knew them myself. She told me that she would get in the lifeboat if there hadn`t been so many people around. So, she and her sons kept together. She was thankful that the three of them had stayed with her on that piece of wreckage. The youngest went first then the other son went. She grew numb and cold and couldn`t remember when she got on the Carpathia. There was a piece of cork in her hair and I managed to get a comb and it took a long time but finally we got it out."[49]

After her arrival in New York, Rosa, who was traveling in a Salvation Army uniform, was received by the

---

[49] www.encyclopedia-titanica.org- Rosa Abbott

Salvation Army and, due to her terrible condition (she was suffering from severe frostbite and her legs were so badly affected by the icy cold that they looked as if they had been burned), was taken to St. Vincent Hospital in New York, where she was kept in a single room away from prying eyes.

Only slowly did Rosa recover from her physical injuries and after some time (some sources speak of over two weeks) she left the hospital with 750 dollars from the Women's Relief Committee and 250 dollars from the TITANIC relief fund as compensation for her terrible ordeal, where many surviving third-class passengers received medical care after the tragedy.

Rosa then stayed in White Plains, New York, until June 1912, where she was still receiving medical treatment.

Although Major Cowan and his wife from the Salvation Army tried to persuade her to return to her family in England, but the trauma she had suffered was too great for her to be able to board a ship again.

In the meantime, the friends of their eldest son Rossmore had held a memorial service on Tuesday, April 23, 1912, at which they sang "Nearer my god, to thee" and prayed the Lord's Prayer.

The principal paid tribute to Rossmore as a *"conscientious student with amiable qualities, whose excellent scholarship was recognized when he received the Anthony Medal on his graduation day at the school..."*[50]

---

[50] www.emcyclopedia-titanica.org- Rosa Abbott

When the MACKAY-BENNETT found Rossmore's body, this medal was in his pocket. It was attached to a watch with the inscription "Oxford St. Grammar School".

Because Rossmore's body was too disfigured to be embalmed, he was buried at sea.

The body of his younger brother Eugene was never found.

In December 1912, she married her former lodger, George Charles William, in Swansea, Massachusetts. The marriage certificate incorrectly stated that it was her first marriage. He was listed as a brass worker, she as a dressmaker.

Rosa and George settled in Jacksonville, Florida, where he worked as a bookbinder. The main reason for the move was that Rosa had contracted chronic asthma from the sinking of the TITANIC and the hours spent in the icy water, and she hoped Florida would be a better climate for her failing health.

She kept in touch with Emily Goldsmith by letter for many years and in a letter to her Rosa wrote about the loss of her two sons and that she had often felt jealous of Emily because of her son Frankie, as she had lost both her sons. But she was convinced that her sons were better off outside this hard world.

She warned Emily, who also wanted to remarry, and advised her to put everything she would receive in her own name so that she would be able to provide for herself if her husband's love faded. (On Sunday, May 2,

126

1914, Emily Goldsmith finally married Harry Illman, see "The Story of Frankie Goldsmith")

Later in the letter, she reported how difficult it was for her husband, Mr. Williams, a silversmith from London, to find work, and she hinted that they might have to move soon. To alleviate her financial problems, she therefore rented out rooms. She signed this letter "Rhoda".

In 1928, Rosa and George moved back to England, which was a very difficult decision for Rosa, as she never wanted to step foot on a ship again!

The plan was to settle George's father's estate in England and then return to Florida. But after George suffered a severe stroke, they decided to stay in their home in Barnes, Surrey. George died in 1938, and Rosa was still living in their home in Barnes when she passed away on Monday, February 18, 1946 at the age of 73.

THE TRAGIC FATE OF THE SKOOG FAMILY

Northern Europe, and Scandinavia in particular, was affected by great poverty towards the end of the 19th century. For many, emigration to the USA was the only way to escape this poverty at the time.

Wilhelm Johansson Skoog, born on Saturday, April 6, 1872 in Forshem, Skaraborg in Sweden, was no exception. As the son of a farmer, he was used to hard work, but saw no way forward in his homeland of Sweden.

On Sunday, June 5, 1898, he married Anna Bernhardina Karlsdotter who was six years older than him and had worked for many years as a maid in various families.

Their son Johan Erik was born on Sunday, June 18, 1899, but died just three months later, on Saturday, September 16, 1899.

Shortly afterwards, on Friday, October 27, 1899, the couple, grieving for their child, moved to Österplana, Hällekis, to settle down there.

However, the couple did not stay there for long. After careful consideration, they decided to follow the example of many of their compatriots and emigrate to the New World to find happiness there.

On Wednesday, April 25, 1900, the two traveled from Göteborg to Hull (England) and on Tuesday, May 8, 1900, they left Liverpool for America on the steamer ULTONIA, arriving in Boston, Massachusetts, on Tuesday, May 15, 1900.

They traveled on to Iron Mountain, Michigan, where a friend of theirs, John Olsson, lived.

Fortunately, unlike many of their compatriots, both could read and write and settled into their new surroundings quite quickly.

In America, four more children were born to Wilhelm and Anna Skoog: Karl Torsten (born on Friday, July 13, 1900), Mabel C. (born on Tuesday, July 22, 1902), Harald V, (born on Wednesday, August 22, 1906) and Margit Elizabeth (born on Thursday, April 14, 1910).

In 1910 they were living at 318 West Street in Iron Mountain and Wilhelm, who had already acquired American citizenship, was working at the Pewabic Mine as an engineer and living with his family near the mine when his eldest son Karl was involved in a serious railroad accident.

As a result of the accident, his son's left leg had to be amputated and his right leg was so badly affected that his toes were also amputated and he was permanently dependent on crutches.

The family left Iron Moutain in 1911 to settle back in Hällekis, Sweden.

However, they, and their children, were already far too accustomed to life in America to adjust to life in Sweden.

They therefore decided to return to Michigan.

Traveling with them to America were Jenny Hendriksson and her cousin Elin Nathalia Pettersson, who was a niece of Wilhelm Skoog.

On Friday, April 5, 1912, the Skoog family, together with Jenny Hendriksson and Elin Nathalia Pettersson, left Göteborg on the Wilson Line steamer CALYPSO and arrived in Hull, England, on Sunday, April 7, 1912.

From there they traveled to Southampton, where they boarded the TITANIC as third-class passengers on Wednesday, April 10, 1912 (ticket number 347088, price £27.18).

After the TITANIC hit the iceberg, the family would certainly not have had an easy time getting to the boat deck with four small children, one of whom was on crutches.

Sadly, the entire Skoog family died when the TITANIC sank and none of their bodies were ever recovered.

The newspaper "The Diamond Drill" from Crystal Falls, Michigan, reported the tragic fate of the Skoog family on April 27, 1912:

„ *Mr. Skoog sold out his property at Iron Mountain last fall and went to Sweden for a visit. If he liked it there, he intended to purchase property and settle in the old country, but the ways of his native land seemed to grow disagreeable to him after so long a time in America, and he decided to return with his family and continue his residence in this country. He sailed on the Titanic and is numbered among the missing.* "[51]

The Skoogs' two relatives also did not survive the tragedy and went down with the ship.

While Elin Pettersson's body was never recovered, Jenny's body was later recovered but remained unidentified for many years.

Her clothing was marked "JH", and Jenny Hendriksson was the only female passenger on board the TITANIC with these initials.

The description of the body includes a so-called "cholera belt"; despite the unusual name, this was simply a long cloth wrapped around the waist for support and warmth and often contained pockets for cash.

Her body was later moved to Halifax and buried in Fairview Cemetery in Halifax, Nova Scotia.

---

[51] Quote: The Diamond Drill, April 27, 1912

THE HAPPY RESCUE OF THE COUTTS FAMILY

The 36-year-old Minnie Coutts (née Trainor) had boarded the TITANIC in Southampton together with her two sons William jr. (aged nine) and Neville (aged three).

Minnie was the daughter of Hugh Trainor, a farmer, and his wife Mary and grew up in a very Catholic household in Ireland.

In the spring of 1902, she married William Coutts, a gold and silver engraver and former soldier from Haddingtonshire (Scotland), in Kent (England) and on Thursday, October 16, 1902, her first son William was born in Chatham, Kent. Six years later, on October 23, 1908, their second son Neville was born in Salisbury, Wiltshire.

Shortly afterwards, they both decided to emigrate to America with their two sons, because the family's financial situation was not the best and they thought they would have a better chance of a good life in America.

Initially, William Coutts emigrated to America alone and built up a new life for his family there so that they could join him as soon as possible.

At the beginning of 1912, he had earned a sufficient amount of money and sent his wife Minnie enough money to book a second-class passage so that she and their two sons could join him in their new home at 143 Fourth Avenue, Brooklyn, New York.

To save money for furnishing her new home in America, Minnie bought third class tickets for herself and her two young sons and then boarded the TITANIC at Southampton on Wednesday, April 10, 1912 (ticket number CA37671, cost £15, 18s).

At the time of the collision, Minnie was asleep in her cabin. As she was a light sleeper, she was woken by the impact, but didn't think much of it at first.

She lay awake in her bed for another 15 minutes before she became restless. She got up, got dressed and left her cabin to see what had happened.

When she stepped out into the corridor, it was already very crowded and she heard some of the passengers talking about lifeboats, while others were carrying all their belongings.

This understandably made Minnie nervous and she immediately returned to her cabin to join her two children.

She woke the two boys up, dressed them and put a lifejacket on them. She then searched the cabin for a vest for herself, but couldn't find one. She finally gave up the search and left her cabin with her two sons without a lifejacket for herself.

Minnie made her way to the public rooms on the steerage, but couldn't find a way to get anywhere near the lifeboats.

She had almost given up hope when a sailor came and said, "Quick, all the women and children to the lifeboats!"

He led her to the boat deck and when she got there, she explained to the sailor that she didn't have a life jacket for herself. An American standing nearby had overheard the conversation and stepped forward, lifted his hat, took off his own lifejacket and gave it to her, saying, "Take my lifejacket, ma'am!"

Then he patted the heads of the two boys and asked Minnie: *"If I go down, please pray for me!*

IN SEVERAL LATER ACCOUNTS, MINNIE COUTTS SAID THAT IT WAS A CREW MEMBER OR OFFICER WHO OFFERED HER HIS OWN LIFE JACKET AND ASKED HER TO PRAY FOR HIM IF HE SANK. YOU CAN SEE HOW MEMORIES CAN CHANGE OVER THE YEARS...

Minnie was on the port side of the ship with her two sons, and second officer Charles Herbert Lightoller was in charge of evacuating them. When she was ready to get into the lifeboat with her children, a typical problem occurred on this side of the sinking ship:

As nine-year-old William Jr. was wearing a straw hat, an officer refused him entry to the boat as he supposedly looked older than nine with this hat and he wanted to classify him as a man and thus condemn him to certain death!

It took Minnie a lot of persuasion to convince the officer that William Jr. was only nine years old and therefore by no means a man. Finally, she said: *"If he doesn't come with us, we won't come either!"*

The officer finally gave in and allowed all three of them to board lifeboat number 2, which, according to Minnie, only had about 17 people on board.

THIS SCENE ALSO SHOWS HOW NONSENSICAL THE ORDER "WOMEN AND CHILDREN FIRST" WAS, IF YOU EXCLUDED THE BOYS.

Minnie Coutts and her sons William Jr. and Neville survived the sinking of the TITANIC and were welcomed back to New York by her relieved husband on the CARPATHIA.

To commemorate his family's survival, father William Coutts engraved a medallion with the names of his two sons and the date of the sinking, containing photos of his wife Minnie and his sons. This medallion is still in the family's possession today.

After the family was happily reunited, they moved after a while to Dormont, Pennsylvania where they lived at 2615 Ocean Avenue.

The elder son William Jr. married Alma Blanch Eiferd, who was born a week after the sinking of the TITANIC and was from Pennsylvania.

They first settled in Dormont, but did not stay there for a long time and moved to Pittsburgh, where they were registered residents in the 1940s.

William Jr. worked as a professional musician for several years - he played guitar and banjo at the William Penn Theatre and also gave music lessons.

He then worked for many years as a manager for the Household Finance Corps before working as a credit manager for the Rubber Products Co. of Pittsburgh. During his career there, he was threatened with a gun six times.

He had two daughters. Fay Alma (1930-1997) and Barbara (born 1932). He was also a member of the Masonic Lodge.

On August 19, 1956, his wife Alma died suddenly at the age of 44 and he became a widower.

On Boxing Day 1957, at the age of 55, William Coutts Jr. suffered a stroke behind the wheel of his car and died in his car on South Water Street in Steubenville, Ohio. He found his final resting place at Sunset View Cemetery in Pittsburgh.

His younger brother Neville was still living with his parents in Dormont, Pennsylvania in 1930 and was a steelworker.

On July 18, 1941, he married Edna Mary Jordan (born June 4, 1910), who was from Pennsylvania. The couple had no children.

Neville later worked as a stock and bond salesman in New York City while maintaining a home in Maplewood, New Jersey and caring for his elderly mother Minnie in her final years.

In 1958, Neville Coutts was one of about a dozen survivors who attended the premiere of the movie "A night to remember" in Manhattan.

His mother Minnie Coutts was widowed in 1956 and had moved to live with Neville. In 1957 she gave several interviews about her experiences on the TITANIC.

On February 29, 1960, Minnie Coutts died at the age of 84 in the home of her son Neville.

Neville and his wife Edna later retired to Florida. He died on March 29, 1977 at the age of 68 in Islamorada, Plantation Key.

By then he had been the last of the three Coutts survivors of the TITANIC.

THANKS

At the end of my fifth TITANIC book, I would like to take the opportunity to thank some important people without whose support this and also my previous books could not have been realized:

I would like to thank my wife Yvonne for the support of my TITANIC passion for many years.

My thanks go to Katharina Becks for her initial proofreading and her great patience in reading that book. She was a great help with some changes in this book.

Many thanks to my proofreader Julie Hanna. She was a great help to realize this English version of my book.

Huge thanks to the British Titanic Society and Clive Sweetingham for their tremendous support and help in researching the story of Leo Zimmermann.

A big thank you goes to David Oliveira for the wonderful cover of the book.

RECOMMEND LITERATURE ON THE TOPIC

Walter Lord
A Night to Remember
ISBN: 978-0-553-27827-9

David Haisman
"I´ll see you in New York"
ISBN 0-6463-3236-8

David Haisman
Raised on the Titanic – An Autobiography
ISBN 0- 646-33265-1

David Haisman
TITANIC – The Edith Brown Story
ISBN: 978-1-4389-6182-8

Donald Lynch, Ken Marshall
Ghosts oft he Abyss
ISBN: 0-306-81223-1

Susan Wels
Titanic: Legacy of the World`s Greatest Ocean Liner
ISBN: 978-0-7835-5261-3

James Cameron
Mission TITANIC
ISBN: 978-3667102393

Lawrence Beesley
The Loss of The SS Titanic

Simon Medhurst
TITANIC Day by Day (366 Days with the TITANIC)
ISBN: 978 139901 143 3

Bill Wormstedt, J. Kent Layton, Tad Fitch
On a sea of glass: The life&loss of the RMS Titanic
ISBN: 978-1445647012

Bill Willard
Our Story
ISBN 978-1-60495-041-0

TITANIC SOCIETIES AND WEBSITES

British Titanic Society

https://www.britishtitanicsociety.com

Deutscher Titanic-Verein von 1997 e.V

https://www.titanicverein.de

Belfast Titanic Society

http://www.belfast-titanic.com

Titanic Verein Schweiz

https://titanicverein.ch

Titanic Historical Society

https://titanichistoricalsociety.org

Titanic Connections

https://www.titanicconnections.com

MORE BOOKS BY THE AUTHOR

TITANIC – Chronology of a Disaster

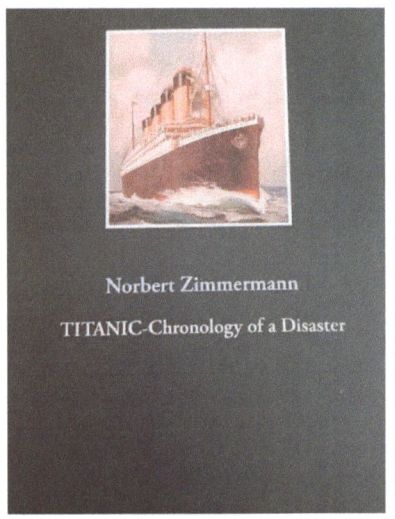

This book tells the story of the TITANIC from its planning and finishing in Belfast, Ireland, to her departure from Southampton. The author of the book also explains the inconsistencies surrounding the collision of the TITANIC with the iceberg and describes what, according to the latest TITANIC research, happened in the last hours before the sinking. The many tragic fates of the tragedy are also dealt with in detail, as well as the later scapegoats of the disaster.

ISBN: 978-3753406473, 370 Pages

The second sinking of the TITANIC

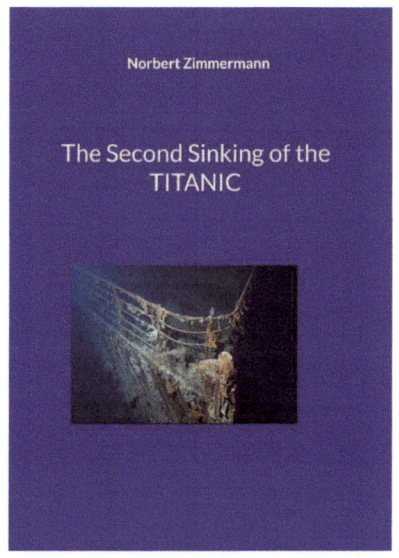

More than one hundred years have passed since the tragic sinking of the TITANIC on April 15, 1912. But the famous ship finds no peace. Many questions are still unanswered. Who really found the wreck of the TITANIC? What is the story behind the open letter to Robert Ballard? What will happen to the recovered artifacts of the TITANIC? This book tries to find answers to these questions and also takes a look into the future.

ISBN : 978-3756257980, 114 Pages